THE WAR OF THE GODS
IN ADDICTION

THE WAR OF THE GODS IN ADDICTION

C. G. Jung, Alcoholics Anonymous, and Archetypal Evil

DAVID E. SCHOEN

 CHIRON PUBLICATIONS • ASHEVILLE, NORTH CAROLINA

www.ChironPublications.com
Previously published by Spring Journal Books

Printed primarily in the United States of America.

ISBN 978-1-63051-920-9 paperback
ISBN 978-1-63051-921-6 hardcover
ISBN 978-1-63051-922-3 electronic
ISBN 978-1-63051-923-0 limited edition paperback

Library of Congress Cataloging-in-Publication Data Pending

Dedication

This book is dedicated to Dorothy, Aggie, Paul, John, Chris, Mary, Bobby, Dave, Wayne, Bette, Dee, Robin, O'Neal, Janice, Linda, Ellen, Joe, Darnell, Roy, and all those in recovery or struggling with addiction issues.

Special thanks go to my brother, Paul Schoen, an addictions counselor, and my good friend Rita Breath, a clinical psychologist, for their feedback, consultation, and helpful suggestions throughout the book.

I'd like to thank Nancy Cater at Spring Journal Books for choosing to publish this book. Thanks also to Robert Freehill for his generosity and encouragement in typing the final drafts of my manuscript, as well as to Sondra Johnson, who worked very hard on the initial draft and revisions. I would also like to acknowledge and thank Sylvia Ruud for her conscientious copy editing. Thanks to Matthew Schoen, my son, for designing the cover, and Peggy, my wife, for being so supportive and giving me the space and time I needed to write and pull all the pieces together and for helping me with "e-mail."

Contents

Author's Note

When *The War of the Gods in Addiction* was first published in 2009, I was hoping it would be a true contribution toward a better understanding of the complex and complicated nature of alcoholism, addiction and recovery. I hoped it would shed light on why the 12 Steps of AA work and why. I hoped it would add to the theoretical exploration of the psychodynamics in the creation of alcoholism and addiction.

In the 11 years since its publication I have presented all over the country and have been immensely gratified and humbled at the reception and validation I and the book have received. My biggest concern was whether what I had written would "hold water" so to speak? Did it ring true to recovering alcoholic and addicted individuals? Did it accurately reflect their experience of addiction, AA and recovery? The response from the recovering 12 Step community has been overwhelmingly affirming. A number of alcoholic individuals have come up to me after reading my book and hearing my presentation to tell me "I don't know how you know what you know about alcoholism and AA but somehow you know it?"

I am not recovering personally from alcoholism and addiction so this was the greatest compliment I could get from the people on the inside who really know because they have lived and experienced it. My book has been used in study groups, book clubs and discussion forums. It has been used as a primary text at Pacifica in California for its course on addiction. I continue to have individuals contact me about the book, its ideas and availability.

I am grateful to Chiron for agreeing to republish *The War of the Gods in Addiction* after it had gone out of print for several years. My previous publisher closed up shop. I have wanted it to continue to be a part of the discussion on alcoholism, addiction, AA and recovery going forward. This reprinting and rerelease assures that it will be! Thank you, Chiron. Deo Gratias!

David Schoen

Preface

This book has evolved gradually over the past thirty years. It is rooted in both my personal and professional experience as an alcohol and chemical dependency counselor, clinical social worker, and Jungian analyst. A number of my siblings and close relatives are recovering alcoholics with many years of sobriety now. Alcoholics Anonymous literally saved their lives when nothing else could touch them. I have the greatest respect for and appreciation of A.A. and the Twelve Steps, because I saw firsthand how my brothers and sisters were lost and now they are found—thanks to A.A. I must confess my bias: that I have very little patience and tolerance for ignorant, theoretical "A.A. bashing" (a number of such books can be found on the shelves of many of the major bookstores), because of my profound personal experience of its powerful effectiveness in changing and transforming individual lives, especially of those I love.

In the process of studying Jungian psychology and becoming a Jungian analyst I realized how little many in the mental health, Jungian, and psychoanalytic communities really know and understand about addiction, and about A.A. and how it works. Conversely, I found a corresponding lack of knowledge and information regarding Jungian psychology on the part of many in the A.A. and recovering communities, even though Carl Jung was such a key figure in the process of the original founding of A.A.

Living in both worlds, I recognized, as Jung did, how much A.A. and Jungian psychology have in common; how similar the Twelve Steps are to the different stages and processes of individuation; how spirituality is central to both; how the relativizing of the ego, its not being the supreme god of the psyche, is the same in both systems, each having its own language for the phenomenon; how similar the concepts of the Self and the Higher Power are; how profoundly both appreciate the absolutely destructive transpersonal qualities of evil— A.A. with its concept of alcoholism and addiction and Jungian psychology with its concept of Archetypal Shadow/Archetypal Evil; and how dreams can greatly assist one on the journey of both addiction recovery and in exploring the vast psychological territory of the unconscious.

Through the years I have lectured and given various workshops and seminars on these subjects. While presenting in Kansas City a number of years ago, I realized that all of the ingredients I needed had been cooking and simmering in one of those gigantic Louisiana gumbo pots on a very low fire in the back of my brain for a very long time. I realized they had finally mixed, melded, and come together enough to create something greater and more integrated than all the separate ingredients— there was a bigger picture, a synthesis, which was now ready to put over brown rice, to serve and to share with others. So in the metaphor of gumbo, I offer you my hopefully well-cooked, ready to imbibe and digest book on the psychodynamics of addiction. In this spirit, I hope it will feed and nourish both the A.A. and recovering communities as well as the mental health, Jungian, and psychoanalytic communities in a process of mutual dialogue, exploration, understanding, appreciation, respect, and service to humanity. I hope it will help individuals struggling with addiction, their families, and their friends in their healing journey of recovery toward the wholeness of their beings.

Introduction

By education and training I am a sociologist, a clinical social worker, a chemical dependency addictions counselor, and a Jungian analyst; by temperament and philosophy I am a "phenomenologist." A phenomenologist is a person whose primary interest is the study of phenomena—the study of things as they actually are. However, I make no special claims to an ability to more objectively or absolutely understand reality or any other phenomenon. My subjectivity, limitedness, blindnesses, and biases are at least equal to, if not greater than, those of others. The only advantage, I believe, in being a phenomenologist is that I hold no fundamentally absolute allegiance or loyalty to any theory or perspective per se, including Jungian psychology. My allegiance to theories or perspectives is only to the extent that they accurately reflect and help me to understand some aspect of a phenomenon or process. The closer a theory is to accurately capturing and reflecting the reality of something, the more value and weight it has for me. The reverse is also true, in that the further away a theory or explanation is from what seems to me to be an accurate representation of what is going on, the less interest I have in it. All theories are hypotheses, maps, or lenses that try to create a picture or a formula that as accurately as possible reflects and represents a phenomenon. Some maps are better than others.

In the arena of alcoholism and addictions, there are many competing and sometimes confusing maps that try to explain the phenomena. Some are more helpful in capturing one aspect of addiction than another. Some maps are so inaccurate that they remind me of the story where the man in the rental car keeps getting hopelessly lost trying to find his way around Detroit until he realizes he's been driving around using a map of Chicago.[1]

In my opinion, all of the present psychodynamic maps of addiction fail to accurately represent the phenomena and account for the essential and unique aspects of addiction that are crucially important in psychologically understanding the nature of addiction and what can be helpful in its treatment. This book will not go into already known history or existing theories regarding the nature of alcoholism and addiction. It will not explore ideas of alcoholism as moral failing or character weakness, or as a symptom of other underlying diseases, physical or psychological.[2] It will not emphasize the *DSM:IV* diagnostic view of alcohol abuse versus dependence, or its similar categorizing of other mood-altering drugs or particular behaviors, as part of the psychiatric view of mental/emotional disorders. It will not explore views of addiction as neurological, hereditary, behavioral, cultural, familial, or social.

This in no way is meant to diminish or devalue the significance or validity of these contributions, theories, ideas, or sources of information. It is worth the considerable time and energy to explore and understand them all, but the intention of this book is not to provide a comprehensive survey of what is already known and written on the addiction landscape, which can already be found in many other places. This book means to break new ground on the subject.

There are elements of alcoholism and addiction that are genetic, hereditary, physiological, neurological, nutritional, biochemical, social, environmental, and cultural. These are all significant pieces to the puzzle of addiction and need to be further explored, studied, and understood. My focus, however, will be only on the psychological— specifically, the psychodynamics of addiction, by which I mean the specific psychic ingredients and psychological processes involved in its creation and development, seen primarily from a Jungian point of view. At this time, I feel that only the Jungian view of the psyche can adequately explain, psychodynamically, the incredible complexity and unique aspects of the addiction and recovery process.

A.A. has intuitively, instinctively, pragmatically, and experientially discovered these dynamics, and addresses them in a very practical, implementable way in its Twelve Steps, but A.A. has never been able adequately to translate its experience into the psychodynamic language spoken by most mental health professionals. I am not criticizing A.A.— their job is to get and keep people sober. They are rightly more concerned about what works than about whether those of us in the psychoanalytic and mental health professions "get it" or not. But it is important that we do "get it," and that this gap between "what works" and "*why* it works" is bridged for the future. The bridge could be a win-win-win for those in active addictions, as well as for the A.A. recovering and mental health communities. Many people's lives will depend upon it.

A.A. has established irrefutably that its Twelve Step Program is, far beyond any other, the most effective and successful treatment approach in getting and keeping alcoholic individuals sober. A.A. has also done a good job in communicating "how" its Twelve Step Program works; what they haven't been able to explain well enough is "why" it works. The "why" is what I want to address in this book, especially for the skeptics, agnostics, and nonbelievers. I believe I can explain why the A.A. program works with addicted individuals when everything else has failed. What is it about this phenomenon of A.A. that makes it different? Why is A.A. effective when other approaches fail? We would ask the same questions if we suddenly found a drug or treatment that cured AIDS or cancer or heart disease; we would want to know how it works and why.

DEFINITION OF ADDICTION

The phenomena I am talking about affects seven percent of the population of alcoholic truly addicted individuals. Research indicates that 20 percent of the population have problem drinking abuse issues.

Let me begin by defining my terms. The first important question is: What is a psychological addiction? Psychologically, addiction is not just a tendency to overindulge in alcohol, drugs, sex, or fudge. Addiction is not laziness, bad habits, or just being human. It is not simply a lack of willpower, motivation, self-discipline, initiative, education, or information. Addiction is not merely an extension of the abuse of substances or behaviors until they become dependencies. It is not merely moral or spiritual character weakness. It is not the inability to resist temptation. It is not just overwhelming appetite or craving; it is more than excessiveness. It is not the use of alcohol or drugs or sex or gambling or food as a temporary response to stress, grief, or a reactive situational depression. It is more than sociopathic superego lacunae. Though many of these factors, elements, and dynamics may be involved in an addiction, they are not sufficient in and of themselves to define or adequately explain it.

My definition of psychological addiction for the purposes of this book has two key components. First, the addictive substance, activity, or behavior must ultimately take over complete and total control of the individual, psychologically. That is, it must take over control of normal ego functioning—thoughts, emotions, perceptions, motivations, judgments, decisions, actions, and behaviors. And the second part of this definition is crucial: the addiction takes over control in an inherently destructive and ultimately life-threatening way. It is not an addiction unless it is a death sentence—not life in prison, not fifty years, with probation or time off for good behavior. It is a death sentence of the mind, of the emotions, of the body, and of the spirit. It is a death sentence to the addict's career, community, marriage, family, and friends. It is not an addiction unless it has the lethal capacity and potential, the power to kill the individual. It is not an addiction unless it is the most powerful, controlling, possessing, dictating, and determining agenda in the psyche. It must take precedence over everything else.

Francis Nemerck, OMI, and Marie Coombs, Hermit, in their book on addiction viewed through the lenses of St. John of the Cross (the great medieval Spanish mystic of "The Dark Night of the Soul" fame) and Pierre Teilhard de Chardin (the great Jesuit philosopher, theologian, and scientist who explored the question of the development and influence of Christ-consciousness upon the biological and spiritual evolution of the cosmos), define addiction in very much the same way as I do:

> Addiction … is a pathological relationship. It uses persons, objects or events for purposes that they cannot possibly fulfill. The addiction becomes the all-absorbing focus, the provider of ultimate meaning, and the sole reason for being of the addict. Everything s/he does revolves increasingly around the object of desire. In that way, the addiction becomes a god to which the addict is completely subjected.[3]

A psychological addiction truly takes possession of the person in the deepest and most sinister sense of "being possessed." I do not use this term in merely an imaginal or metaphorical sense.

There are medical definitions of addiction that use biological and physiological criteria—dealing with changes in the body, structurally and biochemically; measuring things such as metabolism, cravings, serotonin uptake, buildup of toxicities, organ deterioration, and so on. Medical, physical definitions of addiction for a long time only addressed substances such as alcohol or drugs. They failed to account for behaviors and activities such as gambling, sex addiction, dysfunctional relationships, overwork, etc. More recent neurological and biochemical research has confirmed that many of the same reactions occur in the brain, nervous system, and physiology in all types of addictions, regardless of whether the addiction is to substances, behaviors, or relationships.

All physical addictions have a psychological behavioral component, but not all physical addictions are also psychological addictions. There can be physical dependence or addiction without psychological addiction per se. There are cases I know of where people were overmedicated during medical treatment or painful surgeries and their bodies became dependent and addicted, usually to pain medication, but their psyches did not. Once physical detox and withdrawal from the pain medication was complete, there was no deep, lingering psychological craving to continue to indulge in the use of the addictive substance. These people were physically addicted but were never really psychologically addicted. Of course there is always an interactional relationship connection between soma (body) and psyche (soul) in a wholistic, yin/yang way. But as interesting as these theoretical, medical, and physical nuances, distinctions, and questions might be, they are not the real focus of this book.

A further note of clarification involves what some people describe as "positive addictions," meaning habits, activities, behaviors, obsessions, possessions, and substances that are viewed as healthy, helpful, life-giving, and spiritually enriching. I use the term "addiction" in this book in the current clinical sense of a negative, destructive dependency, as pathology—and not in the older Latin sense of "addictus," as in "devoted to" someone or something, where the meaning could be positive, such as one being addicted to the service or love of God, etc. Once again, as interesting and fascinating as it might be to digress, the main objective and focus of this book is a more accurate, comprehensive psychodynamic explanation of addiction. On this basis, the term "positive addictions" is not helpful for our purposes, because it only confuses and muddies the waters of diagnosis and discernment when we describe good habits as addictions. Jogging, falling in love, gardening, being a sports fan, fishing, praying, or watching your diet are not addictions. Nor is being well organized (anal), hyper, or highly opinionated. None of these is a death sentence. They do not fit the ultimately destructive, life-threatening criteria of a true psychological addiction. If everything is an addiction, then nothing is an addiction, and the term becomes so overused, generalized, and watered down it becomes meaningless and of no use in a clinical sense to help describe and understand the phenomenon.

The following example illustrates the problem that this kind of definition-confusion can bring. Gerald May's book *Addiction and Grace: Love and Spirituality in the Healing of Addictions* is wrestling with some of these same questions about healing and addiction. May agrees that all addictions are bad, and that what is necessary to address addiction is a transcendent spiritual force that he simply calls "grace":

> Understanding will not deliver us from addiction, but it will, I hope, help us appreciate grace. Grace is the most powerful force in the universe. It can transcend repression, addiction and every other internal or external power that seeks to oppress the freedom of the human heart. Grace is where our hope lies.[4]

Grace, for May, equals the Higher Power of A.A., which equals the Self in Jungian psychology, and I believe he is on the right track with this idea. My problem with May's approach is his definition of addiction as "any compulsive, habitual behavior that limits the freedom of human desire."[5] He does not distinguish between mere bad habits and behaviors that have the potential to kill you. He sees everyone as suffering from addiction, as part of the human condition. This approach may be democratic and inclusive of all humanity, but it really isn't helpful in understanding the phenomenon of clinical, pathological addiction and the psychodynamic processes involved.

It is necessary to contrast and compare phenomena to better understand them, and when someone claims a phenomenon is so common and universal that it is everywhere in everyone all the time, then how can we define it as anything but human nature in general? May includes, under his categories of attraction addictions, popcorn and chocolate, and under aversion addictions, mice and success. His view of addiction has the potential to subsume every mental illness, pleasure, relationship, and activity there is. Once again, logically, if addiction is everything, everywhere, all the time, then it is either some form of pan-divinity or else it is just as well nothing, nowhere, because we will never be able to distinguish it, if it is everything, from anything else.

This does not do justice to the true nature of addiction, and actually makes it easier to ignore or dismiss true addiction as a real phenomenon. Perhaps most importantly, May does not appreciate the Archetypal Shadow/Archetypal Evil aspect of addiction as a transpersonal, trans-ego factor in the dynamics of addiction. I do want to acknowledge May's contribution to further exploring and understanding the psychological nature of addiction and recovery in general. His appreciation for the transpersonal elements of addiction, especially in recovery, is a valid and helpful description of the phenomena, particularly the fact that there are archetypal implications.

In Chapter Three I will go into more detail about why this destructive, life-threatening aspect is crucial to the definition of addiction and its understanding. My position on the definition of addiction is not meant to be arbitrary or autocratic. I am not indulging in semantic mind-play to be argumentative. I am not trying to usurp the word and its meaning, but to describe a fundamentally important phenomenon for which we most often use the term addiction. What is really important is not the label, but the essential understanding of the characteristics of the phenomenon. If there were a less confusing, more user-friendly word to do it justice I happily would use it. In the meantime I will use the term addiction and will point out when the term is being used in ways other than to describe what I am trying to understand.

The format of this book is as follows: Chapter One will examine the profound implications of the Bill W./Carl Jung correspondence in guiding the focus, direction, and conclusions for the rest of the book. Chapter Two will trace the psychodynamic development of the process of a typical addiction, using the Jungian view of the psyche to shed light on numerous aspects of the process of what I call the Addiction-Shadow-Complex, and constantly referring back to the A.A. experience of alcoholism, the Twelve Steps, and recovery. Chapter Three will delineate the crucial component in addiction—Archetypal Shadow/Archetypal Evil—exploring what it is and how it operates; examining its reflections in fairy tales, myth, and religion, as well as its existence in other clinical theories and formulations. Whenever I use the combined terms Archetypal Shadow/Archetypal Evil in this book, they are meant to be understood to be synonymous with each other, to have the same meaning. I use both terms because some people are more attuned to one usage or the other, and I believe the two terms together better reflect the nuances of the phenomena I intend to describe.

Chapter Four will explore the road to recovery through the healing process outlined in the Twelve Steps of A.A., and how the steps correspond to the different psychodynamic stages of recovery from a Jungian perspective. Chapter Five looks at the significance of the "using dreams" of alcoholic and addicted individuals during different stages of their recovery, and how the "using dreams" can be helpful to them in diagnosis, prognosis, and treatment.

The final section is the conclusion and my final thoughts.

CHAPTER ONE

Setting the Stage:
The Bill W. – Carl Jung Letters

BILL W.'S LETTER

January 23, 1961
Professor Dr. C. G. Jung
Küsnacht-Zürich
Seestrasse 228
Switzerland

My dear Dr. Jung:

This letter of great appreciation has been very long overdue.

May I first introduce myself as Bill W., a co-founder of the Society of Alcoholics Anonymous. Though you have surely heard of us, I doubt if you are aware that a certain conversation you once had with one of your patients, a Mr. Roland H., back in the early 1930's, did play a critical role in the founding of our fellowship.

Though Roland H. has long since passed away, the recollection of his remarkable experience while under treatment by you has definitely become part of A.A. history. Our remembrance of Roland H.'s statements about his experience with you is as follows:

Having exhausted other means of recovery from his alcoholism, it was about 1931 that he became your patient. I believe he remained under your care for perhaps a year. His admiration for you was boundless, and he left you with a feeling of much confidence.

To his great consternation, he soon relapsed into intoxication. Certain that you were his "court of last resort," he again returned to your care. Then followed the conversation between you that was to become the first link in the chain of events that led to the founding of Alcoholics Anonymous.

My recollection of his account of that conversation is this: First of all, you frankly told him of his hopelessness, so far as any further medical or psychiatric treatment might be concerned. This candid and humble statement of yours was beyond doubt the first foundation stone upon which our Society has since been built.

Coming from you, one he so trusted and admired, the impact upon him was immense.

When he then asked you if there was any other hope, you told him that there might be, provided he could become the subject of a spiritual or religious experience—in short, a genuine conversion. You pointed out how such an experience, if brought about, might remotivate him when nothing else could. But you did caution, though, that while such experiences had sometimes brought recovery to alcoholics, they were, nevertheless, comparatively rare. You recommended that he place himself in a religious atmosphere and hope for the best. This I believe was the substance of your advice.

Shortly thereafter, Mr. H. joined the Oxford Group, an evangelical movement then at the height of its success in Europe, and one with which you are doubtless familiar. You will remember their large emphasis upon the principles of self-survey, confession, restitution, and the giving of oneself in service to others. They strongly stressed meditation and prayer. In these surroundings, Roland H. did find a conversion experience that released him for the time being from his compulsion to drink.

Returning to New York, he became very active with the "O.G." here, then led by an Episcopal clergyman, Dr. Samuel Shoemaker. Dr. Shoemaker had been one of the founders of that movement, and his was a powerful personality that carried immense sincerity and conviction.

At this time (1932-34), the Oxford Group had already sobered a number of alcoholics, and Roland, feeling that he could especially identify with these sufferers, addressed himself to the help of still others. One of these chanced to be an old schoolmate of mine, named Edwin T. ["Ebby"]. He had been threatened with commitment to an institution, but Mr. H. and another ex-alcoholic "O.G." member procured his parole, and helped to bring about his sobriety.

Meanwhile, I had run the course of alcoholism and was threatened with commitment myself. Fortunately, I had fallen under the care of a physician—a Dr. William D. Silkworth— who was wonderfully capable of understanding alcoholics. But just as you had given up on Roland, so had he given me up. It was his theory that alcoholism had two components—an obsession that compelled the sufferer to drink against his will and interest, and some sort of metabolism difficulty which he then called an allergy. The alcoholic's compulsion guaranteed that the alcoholic's drinking would go on, and the allergy made sure that the sufferer would finally deteriorate, go insane, or die. Though I had been one of the few he had thought it possible to help, he was finally obliged to tell me of my hopelessness; I, too, would have to be locked up. To me, this was a shattering blow. Just as Roland had been made ready for his conversion experience by you, so had my wonderful friend Dr. Silkworth prepared me.

Hearing of my plight, my friend Edwin T. came to see me at my home, where I was drinking. By then, it was November 1934. I had long marked my friend Edwin for a hopeless case. Yet here he was in a very evident state of "release," which could by no means be accounted for by his mere association for a very short time with the Oxford Group. Yet this obvious state of release, as distinguished from the usual depression, was tremendously convincing. Because he was a kindred sufferer, he could unquestionably communicate with me at great depth. I knew at once that I must find an experience like his, or die.

Again I returned to Dr. Silkworth's care, where I could be once more sobered and so gain a clearer view of my friend's experience of release, and of Roland H.'s approach to him.

Clear once more of alcohol, I found myself terribly depressed. This seemed to be caused by my inability to gain the slightest faith. Edwin T. again visited me and repeated the simple Oxford Group formulas. Soon after he left me, I became even more depressed. In utter despair, I cried out, "If there be a God, will He show Himself." There immediately came to me an illumination of enormous impact and dimension, something which I have since tried to describe in the book *Alcoholics Anonymous* and also in *AA Comes of Age*, basic texts which I am sending to you.

My release from the alcohol obsession was immediate. At once, I knew I was a free man.

Shortly following my experience, my friend Edwin came to the hospital, bringing me a copy of William James's *Varieties of Religious Experience*. This book gave me the realization that most conversion experiences, whatever their variety, do have a common denominator of ego collapse at depth. The individual faces an impossible dilemma. In my case, the dilemma had been created by my compulsive drinking, and the deep feeling of hopelessness had been vastly deepened still more by my alcoholic friend when he acquainted me with your verdict of hopelessness respecting Roland H.

In the wake of my spiritual experience, there came a vision of a society of alcoholics, each identifying with and transmitting his experience to the next—chain style. If each sufferer were to carry the news of the scientific hopelessness of alcoholism to each new prospect, he might be able to lay every newcomer wide open to a transforming spiritual experience. This concept proved to be the foundation of such success as Alcoholics Anonymous has since achieved. This has made conversion experience—nearly every variety reported by James—available on almost wholesale basis. Our sustained recoveries over the last quarter-century number about 300,000. In America and through the world, there are today 8,000 AA groups.

So to you, to Dr. Shoemaker of the Oxford Group, to William James, and to my own physician, Dr. Silkworth, we of AA owe this tremendous benefaction. As you will now clearly see, this astonishing chain of events actually started long ago in your consulting room, and it was directly founded upon your own humility and deep perception.

Very many thoughtful AAs are students of your writings. Because of your conviction that man is something more than intellect, emotion, and two dollars' worth of chemicals, you have especially endeared yourself to us.

How our Society grew, developed its Traditions for unity, and structured its functioning, will be seen in the texts and pamphlet material that I am sending you.

You will also be interested to learn that, in addition to the "spiritual experience," many AAs report a great variety of psychic phenomena, the cumulative weight of which is very considerable. Other members have—following their recovery in AA—been much helped by your practitioners. A few have been

intrigued by the *I Ching* and your remarkable introduction to
that work.

　　Please be certain that your place in the affection, and in
the history, of our Fellowship is like no other.

Gratefully yours,

William G. W————[1]

B ill W., one of the cofounders of A.A., wrote this remarkable letter of deepest appreciation to Carl Jung, dated January 23,
1961, thanking Dr. Jung for his part "in the chain of events
that led to the founding of Alcoholics Anonymous." Dr. Jung responded to Bill W.'s letter on January 30, 1961—one week later. These
two letters contain a wealth of previously unknown information and
insight about A.A., its history, the dynamics of alcoholism, and Jung's
views on the subject—and by extension his views on addiction dynamics in general. Within these two letters are the seeds and outline
of this entire book, the template for expansion and extrapolation of
Jung's and A.A.'s basic views of alcoholism, its psychodynamics and
its effective treatment.

　　Without these letters, we would have next to nothing of Jung's
core ideas on alcoholism and addiction. The fact that the letters were
written in January 1961, only a short five months before Jung's death
on June 6, 1961, gives them great historical significance in the sense
that Jung's response, being at the very end of his life, reflects the cul-
mination and synthesis of his thoughts on the subject. It is a conclud-
ing summary from his incredible life experience and work and a direct, frank formulation of what he truly thought was going on in alcoholism and addiction. It is one of the last communications before
his death. In a sense, it is his final will and testament on the subject.

　　In Jung's collected works there are twenty-eight references to alcoholism. The majority are early references related to the description
of patient subjects who participated in his groundbreaking word association experiments between 1904 and 1909, which established
scientifically and empirically the existence of the unconscious and of
the emotionally charged autonomous phenomena of psychological
complexes, previously only postulated by Sigmund Freud. He makes
one reference to a short-lived conversion to sobriety of a man "cured
by Jesus" through a group religious experience.[2] Most of his comments

and references to alcoholism present it as one of the worst, most debilitating and degenerative mental illnesses possible. There is a sense of hopelessness about the condition reflected in the prevailing medical, scientific, and mental health communities' views of alcoholism in the early 1900s as an incurable and untreatable disease. The failure of any and all treatment approaches, including psychoanalysis, resulted in this attitude of resignation, and the despair of helping those unfortunate enough to be stricken by "the curse of alcoholism." It was truly a death sentence—just a matter of time, sooner or later, until it would take one's life. Jung obviously had had the same frustrating failures as everyone else in trying to help his alcoholic patients to stop drinking and reclaim their lives.

Into this socio-medical matrix in 1931 came Roland H., "a young, talented and wealthy financial wizard [who] found himself on the verge of despair over his inability to control his drinking. Having attempted virtually every other 'cure,' he turned to one of the greatest medical and psychiatric talents of the time, traveling to Zurich, Switzerland, to place himself under the care of Dr. Carl Gustav Jung."[3] Roland worked with Dr. Jung for approximately a year and was able initially to establish his sobriety. He left treatment with confidence and high hopes of being cured of his addiction. A short time later, like so many alcoholics before and after him, he relapsed into uncontrollable drinking once again. It seemed that even with perhaps the best psychoanalyst in the world helping him it wasn't enough. Ego-insight, awareness of his developmental history, and his exploration of his personal complexes and shadow issues were still not enough to sustain his sobriety. Making the unconscious conscious was not sufficient in and of itself to cure him. Psychoanalysis was not and is not a cure for alcoholism. Multiply Roland's experience by thousands or millions, and you have the disappointing story, over and over again, of the inability of medical, psychiatric, psychoanalytic, and psychotherapeutic efforts to help those suffering from alcoholism to get and stay sober.

Professionals do not like being powerless and mystified, so they begin to blame the patients for not getting better by labeling them "uncooperative," "resistant to treatment," "unmotivated," or "constitutionally untreatable." Suffering alcoholic individuals who were dying from this affliction were now being stigmatized, judged and condemned for not being cured. No wonder there has been a longstanding uneasy, untrusting sense on the part of alcoholic and addicted individuals that the professionals, medical and otherwise, didn't really understand them or know what to do. Professionals would take their money, but they didn't help, and often were just full of ignorance and arrogance.

Roland H. returned to Dr. Jung hoping that something else might be tried. He believed in Jung and had great confidence in his ability, judgment, and recommendations. In a refreshing and surprising admission by Jung, summarized in Bill W.'s letter to him, Jung told Roland that his situation was essentially hopeless "so far as any further medical or psychiatric treatment might be concerned." This must have been a devastating blow for Roland that even the great Dr. Jung was powerless over alcohol and that there was no ego-centered insight therapy that could help him. Bill W. credits Jung's "candid and humble statement" as the "first foundation stone upon which our Society (A.A.) has since been built." Bill W. is obviously referring to the now famous Step One of A.A.: "We admitted we were powerless over alcohol—that our lives had become unmanageable." Jung admitted both his and Roland's powerlessness over alcohol, unknowingly taking Step One of A.A. together. Roland inquired if there might be any other hope, and Jung replied that "there might be, provided he could become the subject of a spiritual or religious experience—in short, a genuine conversion." Jung, in this advice to Roland, was encouraging him to submit himself to a spiritual principle that would replace the ego as the center of his consciousness and to seek a transcendent center—which many call God, some call the Universe, Jungians call the Self, and A.A. refers to as the Higher Power. Jung had, intuitively, in effect advised Roland to take Step Two of A.A.: "Came to believe that a Power greater than ourselves could restore us to sanity." The only hope was in giving up hope that Roland could somehow cure himself.

Jung was not sure, and cautioned Roland that "while such experiences had sometimes brought recovery to alcoholics, they were, nevertheless, comparatively rare." Perhaps Jung was thinking of the man "cured by Jesus" mentioned previously, and how, even in that instance, it didn't last. In any case, Jung had probably observed enough seeming miracles occur when the ego psychologically surrendered to the Self (or Higher Power) that he believed that that was Roland's last best chance to avoid being destroyed by his addiction. Jung, at that time, still did not have proof that this surrender would work with alcoholics, but he intuited the truth, and had the daring and courage to send Roland off on a pilgrimage in search of a spiritual transformation.

Roland found and joined the Oxford Group, which was an evangelical religious movement of that time, emphasizing "the principles of self-survey, confession, restitution, and the giving of oneself in service to others. They strongly stressed meditation and prayer." The essence of these principles was adopted by A.A. and reflects many aspects of steps four through twelve—making a searching and fearless inventory; admitting to God, to oneself, and to another the exact nature of one's wrongs; making amends to people harmed; continuing to pray and meditate; and helping other alcoholics in their journey to recovery. With these core principles of the Oxford Group, later to become the steps of A.A., Roland did have his "conversion experience" and was released for a time from his compulsion to drink. A good number of alcoholics were successfully sobering up through the principles of the Oxford Group at the time. The problem was that the Oxford Group didn't know what to do with relapse into alcoholism, and wound up excluding those who couldn't maintain sobriety and their standards. The founders of A.A. learned much from the Oxford Group, including the dangers of perfectionism and the importance of tolerance, as well as group- and self-forgiveness. A.A. never gives up on anyone, no matter what! The addicted person may give up on himself, some do, but the program never gives up hope.

I know of one alcoholic individual who picked up 106 Desire Chips over a twenty-year period of trying to get and stay sober. A Desire Chip is given when a person comes to an A.A. meeting with no sobriety but only a desire to stop drinking (which is all A.A. requires for participation). This individual's lack of success for twenty years probably seemed hopeless, and was certainly frustrating and disappointing for him and those who cared about him, but the reality is that, after so many failures over so many years, he did get sober and stayed sober for twenty-one years, until his death. Some people view every recovering alcoholic as an unbelievable miracle story.

Roland instinctively realized his need to share the miraculous truths of his newfound sobriety with others—this later became known as Step Twelve of A.A.: bringing the message of hope to other alcoholics—and he helped Edwin T. ("Ebby") to get sober. Ebby was a friend of Bill W., and was instrumental through his Twelve Step work in helping Bill W. to get sober.

Bill W., in his letter to Jung, describes his own profound conversion experience, where he was released immediately from his obsession with drinking: "At once, I knew I was a free man." Bill W. realized, after reading William James's *Varieties of Religious Experience*, "that most conversion experiences, whatever their variety, do have a common denominator of ego collapse at depth." In Jungian terms, this phenomenon is referred to as the relativizing of the ego in service to the Self. It is experienced as a tremendous deflation of the ruling principle of the ego and its agendas in deference to a wider, deeper, more comprehensive agenda, to be discovered and discerned in relation to the Self. This phenomenon is expressed in A.A. as ego surrender to the Higher Power ("Let go and let God," "Turn it over"). In religious terms, it is often referred to as submitting to the will of God or the dictates of the Holy Spirit, or becoming one with the Buddha within, or connecting with one's Christ-consciousness, or being open to what Fate or the Universe has in store for us. What is important here is not the label, but the reality of the phenomenon experienced.

Dr. William Silkworth, who specialized in working with alcoholics, was also instrumental in helping to get Bill W. on the road to sobriety. He wrote the first "Doctor's Opinion" section of what is referred to as the Big Book (or Bible) of Alcoholics Anonymous. His experience echoes these same ideas and concepts, only in a more medical, less psychological or spiritual, formulation. He says, "Unless this person (the alcoholic) can experience an entire psychic change, there is very little hope of his recovery." He goes on to say, "One feels that something more than human power is needed to produce the essential psychic change."[4] Dr. Silkworth is clearly implying that there is a power beyond human power that is essential in creating the psychic change, but he declines to name it.

Bill W., in his letter, goes on to talk about the phenomenal success A.A. was having—over 300,000 previously hopeless, incurable alcoholics sober and recovering in 1961 (by now, millions). He acknowledges Dr. Samuel Shoemaker (one of the founders of the Oxford Group), William James, and Dr. Silkworth, along with Dr. Jung, as major founding contributors to the development of the Fellowship of Alcoholics Anonymous. He closes his letter to Dr. Jung indicating his deep appreciation for Dr. Jung's grasp of the reality of "spiritual experience," which Bill W. saw as the cornerstone of recovery in A.A. He mentions many A.A. members' experience of "psychic phenomena," which Jung wrote about as synchronicity—an acausal connecting principle linking seemingly chance external events to an individual at a specific time in a profoundly meaningful subjective way. He also adds that, following their recovery in A.A., a number of A.A. members have been helped on their journey by working on themselves in Jungian analysis. Bill W. ends his letter with heartfelt thanks to Dr. Jung when he says, "Please be certain that your place in the affection, and in the history, of our Fellowship is like no other." These words must have warmed the heart of an aging seeker of truth who would know, shortly before his death, of some of the unknowing good he had done in his life, which was making a difference in the healing and recovery of hundreds of thousands of people. I am sure that Bill W.'s letter was "very welcome indeed" to Jung, a few months before his death. It is unfortunate that Bill W. and Carl Jung did not have the chance to meet and get to know each other. My sense is that they would have very much liked each other and been fast friends—two great minds, two great hearts, two seekers of truth, two men committed to the healing of the human soul. I would love to have been a fly on the wall listening when they talked!

As one can clearly see, the seeds of the first three steps of A.A. were planted by Jung and Roland's failed analysis. The spirit of all the steps of A.A., to speak the unvarnished truth, was modeled by Jung's owning of his limitations and sending Roland off on a quest for a spiritual experience, which was, at best, a long shot. Roland "got the program," as they say in A.A., but sadly, he couldn't hold onto it. Nevertheless, without Jung, and Roland as the messenger, the synchronicities that resulted in the founding of A.A. might never have occurred. And if Bill W. had never written his letter to Carl Jung before Jung's death, which resulted in Jung's sharing his groundbreaking and controversial views on alcoholism, we might never have known about Jung's understanding of crucial aspects of the psychodynamics of addiction, and this present book would never have been conceived or written. Never underestimate the web that holds and connects us all in the most mysterious ways.

Carl Jung's Letter

Küsnacht-Zürich
Seestrasse 228
January 30, 1961

Mr. William G. W——
Alcoholics Anonymous
Box 459 Grand Central Station
New York 17, New York

Dear Mr. W.:

Your letter has been very welcome indeed.

I had no news from Roland H. any more and often wondered what has been his fate. Our conversation which he has adequately reported to you had an aspect of which he did not know. The reason that I could not tell him everything was that those days I had to be exceedingly careful of what I said. I had found out that I was misunderstood in every possible way. Thus I was very careful when I talked to Roland H. But what I really thought about was the result of many experiences with men of his kind.

His craving for alcohol was the equivalent, on a low level, of the spiritual thirst of our being for wholeness, expressed in medieval language: the union with God.*

How could one formulate such an insight in a language that is not misunderstood in our days?

The only right and legitimate way to such an experience is that it happens to you in reality, and it can only happen to you when you walk on a path which leads you to higher understanding. You might be led to that goal by an act of grace or through a personal and honest contact with friends, or through a higher education of the mind beyond the confines of mere rationalism. I see from your letter that Roland H. has chosen the second way, which was, under the circumstances, obviously the best one.

I am strongly convinced that the evil principle prevailing in this world leads the unrecognized spiritual need into perdition if it is not counteracted either by real religious insight or by the protective wall of human community. An ordinary man, not protected by an action from above and isolated in society, cannot resist the power of evil, which is called very aptly the

Devil. But the use of such words arouses so many mistakes that
one can only keep aloof from them as much as possible.

These are the reasons why I could not give a full and sufficient explanation to Roland H., but I am risking it with you
because I conclude from your very decent and honest letter that
you have acquired a point of view above the misleading plati-
tudes one usually hears about alcoholism.

You see, "alcohol" in Latin is *spiritus*, and you use the same
word for the highest religious experience as well as for the most
depraving poison. The helpful formula therefore is: *spiritus contra spiritum.*

Thanking you again for your kind letter
I remain
yours sincerely
C. G. Jung[5]

*"As the hart panteth after the water brooks, so panteth my soul
after thee, O God." (Psalm 42, 1)

Bill W.'s letter must have been important to Jung, because he answered
it almost immediately. Jung's letter is dated exactly seven days after
Bill W.'s (January 23, 1961, and January 30, 1961). Considering the
time it would take for a letter to go from New York to Switzerland,
Jung probably wrote his response and mailed it back to Bill W. as soon
as he received it. He wrote it in the middle of the Christmas-New Year's
holiday season; without delay, with what could be speculated as an
urgency on his part to communicate something very important in this
letter before his death.

Jung's letter is briefer than Bill W.'s, but just as significant, packed
with important information and groundbreaking ideas about his fundamental views on alcoholism and addiction. Jung begins by indicating that the letter from Bill W. was "very welcome indeed." He says
that he had lost touch with Roland H. and had "often wondered"
what had become of him. He affirms that Bill W.'s version of what
happened between Jung and Roland was accurately reported. Jung
goes on to reveal how misunderstood he found himself at that earlier
time, and how "exceedingly careful" he felt he had to be in dealing
with Roland's situation. He could not at that time reveal all of what
he thought and felt and wanted to say to Roland about his alcoholism. He goes on to say that, based on his many experiences with alco-

holics, what he had found, which he was now willing to risk revealing at the very end of his life, was that Roland's craving for alcohol was a low-level thirst for spiritual wholeness, a misplaced worship on the altar of a false idol, but nonetheless an urge, a hunger and thirst for the real thing, not coca cola, but a true "union with God."

Jung refers to his hesitancy to say this for fear of his being misunderstood and misrepresented by others. The people who would potentially misunderstand him were his colleagues in the scientific medical and psychiatric communities, as well as those who would want to concretize and oversimplify what he was saying into some kind of moral condemnation of alcoholism and addiction. His peers might accuse him of abandoning sound scientific and psychological principles for an unsubstantiated "religious" formulation that could be a setback for the young science of psychology back into the murky, magical dark ages of explaining phenomena on the basis of tradition, unquestioned authority, faith, suspicion, and religious orthodoxy. This could be threatening to those who identified themselves with science, who had struggled to legitimize psychology, to separate it from the quacks of pseudo-religion, and religion itself. And then there were those who would take his words and do with them exactly what was most feared—distort them beyond recognition, using them for their own purposes and agendas.

Jung himself was very sensitive about being given a credible hearing by his fellow professionals, as so many of his ideas and concepts already challenged them to the limits of their capacities. For him to begin to make overt psychological statements about God and the Devil would have been just too much. The A.A. community can well appreciate Jung's position, as they have been repeatedly misunderstood by outsiders as a new religion, a cult, a brainwashing organization, an addiction substitute, or anything except the most successful treatment approach for alcoholic and addicted individuals in human history.

In contrast to these misunderstanding projections and distortions of A.A. as cult and brainwashing, one of the key ingredients valued in both A.A. and Jungian psychology is respect for individual personal freedom—to choose to join and participate or not, voluntarily, without being forced, penalized, or coerced. It's always a person's right to stay or to leave A.A. or the Jungian community. No one is required to even speak at an A.A. meeting if they don't want to. A person is free to walk out the door at any time for any reason. Jungian psychology has always acknowledged that it was not for everyone, and A.A. has always emphasized that its membership and participation are by welcome attraction—not by recruitment, solicitation, marketing, or coercion. If you want what you see embodied, lived out, and practiced by recovering members of A.A. or by people on their individuation path informed by Jungian psychology, then you may be interested in finding out more about what they are doing, why, and how it works for them. You always reserve the right to your reservations. Perhaps the passion and enthusiasm you might see demonstrated by these folks—that is mistaken sometimes for brainwashing, cult, religion, or substitute addiction—is in actuality the overwhelmingly grateful appreciation of people for something that has actually saved their lives.

In contrast to dogmatic formulations or unquestioned cult authority, A.A. and Jungian psychology rely upon the guidance of the Higher Power and of the Self, as discerned by the individual from his or her own experiences. A.A. has always advised: "Do what works for you." The principles of the Twelve Steps and the psychodynamics of Jungian psychology, as well as structures and principles found in other systems and programs,[6] can be used as helpful aids in this discernment. Personal human freedom is never questioned by A.A. or Jungian psychology. In fact, A.A. never tells anyone they "cannot have a drink" if they want one; it merely informs them, through A.A.'s experience of the possible or probable consequences of having that drink, and then says, "It's your choice." A.A. and Jungian psychology are not interested in cultivating true-believer robotic clones in any way whatsoever.

The tension and conflict Jung experienced, and which is shared by A.A. to this day, is how to describe the phenomena of addiction and the successful path to recovery accurately and authentically, without referring to these psychologically and societally loaded and controversial aspects of the phenomena, which have only been described in what historically have been spiritual and religious terms imbedded in sectarian religious teachings. A.A. and Jung both tried to adopt more neutral, inclusive language to describe the phenomena, so as to avoid accusations of psychological bias, sectarian allegiance, or some form of church evangelization. A.A. adopted the concept of the Higher Power to describe these realities. Jung went with the Self and the archetypes as the central aspects of the psyche to represent these universal spiritual and psychological principles.

My guess is that Jung was very gratified to get Bill W.'s letter, which supported and verified his previously publicly unexpressed views about alcoholism, addiction, and recovery. The success of A.A. and the thousands of sober alcoholics were living proof, an irrefutable testament of scientific fact, which gave credibility to Jung's views, no longer unproven or needing to be hidden. A.A.'s thousands of sober members, previously untreatable unfortunates, were living proof to Jung, to the world, and to his colleagues that he was right about this phenomenon. However you describe it, the understanding of addiction must incorporate spiritual, transcendent elements to adequately explain the addiction and recovery process. Jung and A.A. both knew and understood this truth.

Both Jungian psychology and A.A. emphasize the spiritual as essential to sobriety, to recovery, and to individuation. They are both very careful not to endorse any one religion or any specific sectarian expression of the spiritual. They both refuse to align with any specific church or religion, while at the same time valuing and honoring principles derived from specific religions and church traditions from all over the world.

I believe A.A. is no more meant to be a new religion than Jungian psychology is, but there are those who have tried to make them both into a kind of religion. The effectiveness of A.A. is not as a religion, but as a recovering therapeutic community. The effectiveness of Jungian psychology is not as a religion, but as a psychology that can help us understand and appreciate our impulses toward the spiritual and what religion has to offer us in this modern world of media, technology, and materialism. Certainly, concepts from A.A. and Jungian psychology can be borrowed by religiously minded individuals to help them on their spiritual journeys. Truth is wherever we find it, whether in the sacred or the secular world. In Chapter Two I will go more in depth into why this spiritual aspect of addiction is truly essential to understanding both the dynamics of addiction and the recovery process.

Jung in his letter to Bill W. goes on to describe the ways in which one might have a personal experience of "union with God" that would bring release from the stranglehold of alcoholism and addiction. This "union with God" would lead to a "higher understanding" of things. Jung suggests this may occur in three ways, as "an act of grace or through a personal and honest contact with friends, or through a higher education of the mind beyond the confines of mere rationalism" (that is, beyond the confines of a consciousness stuck in rational, provable, logical, ego-centered ways of looking at and understanding everything). What is remarkable about Jung's statement here is that he has summarized once again essential components of the A.A. program. For A.A. to work and for sobriety to continue, a person must experience an "act of grace," whether dramatic or subtle—what Dr. Harry M. Tiebout calls a "psychological conversion experience,"[7] which he wrote about fairly extensively beginning in the 1940s. In A.A. this is often talked about as "hitting bottom," when there is a fundamental shift of the conscious ego position and a person is suddenly open, often unexpectedly, to a whole new way of looking at him- or herself and the issue of drinking. This "act of grace" is often the impetus for alcoholic individuals to take Step One of A.A., to admit that they are powerless over alcohol and that their lives have become unmanageable. In Jungian psychology, this experience is what is meant by the relativizing of the ego in relation to the Self.

Jung then goes on to describe the fellowship aspect of A.A. in noting the "personal and honest contact with friends" that is the antidote to alcoholism and addiction. What strikes most people about an A.A. meeting is the level of direct, honest, and personal sharing that goes on in the most loving and nonjudgmental way. The loneliness, alienation, and self-loathing of most alcoholics finds in the fellowship of A.A. a level of acceptance and caring and friendship never experienced before.

Jung's saying that recovery is "through a higher education of the mind beyond the confines of mere rationalism" describes the component of the A.A. program reflected in working the Twelve Steps, having a sponsor, and reading the literature, especially the Big Book of A.A. This is also one of the avenues he sees as available to achieve the "union with God" that leads to the arresting of the addiction.

Jung did not put these three components together—the "act of grace," "personal and honest contact," and "the higher education of the mind"—as the formula for the program of A.A. He was describing from his understanding and experience the three major ways he knew of that people could access the "union with God" necessary for recovery from alcoholism and addiction. He came independently to the same conclusions as A.A. One needs to turn it over to the Higher Power (act of grace), be an active part of the Fellowship (personal and honest contact with friends), and work the Twelve Steps (the higher education of the mind). A.A.'s simplest version of this prescription is "Don't drink, go to meetings, and read the Big Book."

Jung then expresses in his letter to Bill W. a seemingly shocking idea, the implications of which reverberate to the archetypal essence of addiction. Jung wrote: "I am strongly convinced that the evil principle prevailing in this world leads the unrecognized spiritual need into perdition if it is not counteracted either by real religious insight or by the protective wall of human community. An ordinary man, not protected by an action from above and isolated in society, cannot resist the power of evil, which is called very aptly the Devil."[8]

Jung is suggesting here an ultimate archetypal battle of the powers of good and evil for the souls of human beings. He is positing, I believe, in these final days of his life, powerful archetypal transpersonal realms of spiritual darkness, evil, and destruction, pitted against the spiritual powers of light and good and healing transformation. His words warn that the naive and unsuspecting "ordinary man" is in danger of being brought to "perdition" by an army of evil vampire-like spirits roaming the world looking for confused, lost souls who are caught in "unrecognized spiritual" desire, which makes them easy prey for these demons of despair and addiction.

These are not the typically encouraging words of Jung's admonition to befriend, accept, and integrate our subjective darkness, our personal shadow, and our imperfect humanness. These words echo a darker, deeper, more ominous reality of an abyss, a black hole that could swallow us up, regardless of whether we are working on ourselves or not. I'm sure that in Roland H.'s analysis with Jung they worked on understanding and integrating personal shadow, but there was something even bigger going on: the addiction, which was beyond personal unconsciousness and personal shadow. Jung sensed the transpersonal quality in addiction and knew ultimately that to treat it required a transpersonal, transcendent, Higher Power/Self medicine. He advised Roland to "become the subject of a spiritual or religious experience—in short, a genuine conversion." Again, I emphasize, this is not Jung encouraging people to become more conscious; it is Jung sounding a warning to wear garlic, carry a wooden stake and crucifix, and encircle yourself in the consecrated bread of the Eucharist—not literally of course, but metaphorically and psychologically. He says, in effect, that we are lost without the counteraction of either "real religious insight" or "by the protective wall of human community." Some people would describe "real religious insight" as the indwelling of the Holy Spirit, or as the connection with the Christ or Buddha within, or as doing the will of Allah or Yahweh or the Father, or as living in the love and truth of the Great Spirit or of the Goddess, etc. The important point is not which religious form we choose, but that we choose. It is crucial that this "real religious insight" is alive in us and full of power and energy to ward off the transpersonal evil energies in the universe, which will otherwise destroy us.

The other antidote Jung refers to is "the protective wall of human community." When we are in truly loving relationships with other people, when we act collectively out of compassion and charity as a community, when we nurture, protect, and pray for each other, it is much harder for transpersonal evil energies to get to us. On the other hand, if we are isolated, separated from the community, angry, un-happy, and vulnerable, it is much easier for these transpersonal evil energies to cull us from the herd, so to speak, and take us down.

Jung goes even further, saying that if we are not "protected by an action from above" and are "isolated in society," we "cannot resist the power of evil." He doesn't say "it's a problem," or "it's dangerous," or "be careful," or "we might not be okay"—he says that without grace and community we are lost; it's hopeless; the game is over; the power of evil will overcome, consume, and destroy us. These words sound more like a railing prophet from the Old Testament or a fundamentalist preacher than a psychologist describing alcoholism and addiction dynamics. I believe Jung wasn't using these words unintentionally, carelessly, or too loosely. I don't believe he was overstating his case for emphasis' sake. I believe he said what he said, the way he said it, because that's exactly what he meant to say. To recovering alcoholics, Jung's words don't sound extreme or strange or exaggerated; they sound like the truth of what they have known and lived and experienced. Without the saving grace of God or the Higher Power and the Fellow-ship of A.A., most of them will tell you they have no doubt that they wouldn't have a snowball's chance in hell. They would be in the clutches of the evil of the addiction, or dead. The idea of transpersonal evil is not so foreign or strange when you have been possessed by it in the form of an addiction, which cares about nothing and no one except feeding its fix until everything and everyone is used up, until it is all sacrificed on the altar of death and destruction.

Jung then adds the nuclear zinger that this "power of evil" is very aptly called "the Devil." He now links the concept of transpersonal evil with the well-known prince of darkness, the ruler (at least in myth) of the organized legions of evil spirits, the personification of the source and the kingdom of the lost damned souls of humanity. Jung knows how shocking, jolting, and challenging what he is saying is. He knows how easily people will misunderstand, take what he is saying in the wrong way, use it in ways he does not intend, and project, distort, and dismiss him, but he goes on record anyway. He is trying to describe something so important, so crucial for humanity, that he is willing to risk the confusion, ridicule, and misunderstanding it will surely generate, as well as the diminishment of his reputation.

To ordinary, nonaddicted people, Jung's words are extremely challenging and perhaps incomprehensible. If the idea of the existence of the Devil and transpersonal evil has been rationalized away as unreal or as archaic theology; if all this sounds too much like a return to philosophical dualism, which we thought we had moved beyond; or if our psychological religious beliefs assert that everything "is" ultimately integratable (or, on the other side, as in Buddhism, it doesn't truly exist), then Jung's assessment is a stumbling block for many.

I cannot reconcile all of these questions and concerns comfortably for everyone. A number of Buddhist practitioners I know have great difficulty with these ideas because of the orientation map they use, which I have great respect for and value immensely. Most people raised in Jewish, Muslim, or Christian traditions do not have as much difficulty with Jung's concepts theoretically because of the inherent duality principle incorporated in the battle of good and evil between God and the Devil in these traditions. Jung is not trying to assert any theology or religious belief principle over any other; he is trying, I believe, to describe the phenomenon in the best way he knows how. He uses an archetypal duality paradigm because it more accurately cap-

tures and reflects the important aspects of addiction and recovery as
he has experienced and observed them.

My guess is that there are ways in Buddhism and other traditions
to explain these phenomena, but I don't know what they are. Perhaps
some phenomena are best imaged by dualistic maps and others by
unified oneness maps, such as in the Buddhist traditions, as some
aspects of phenomena are better formulated by either monotheistic
or polytheistic formulations or by a combination of both. Perhaps on
the human level and the transpersonal archetypal level fundamental
oppositions still exist, but there are levels somewhere beyond these,
in other realms, that reconcile them into oneness. I do not know the
answer to this question.

But, for now, to understand the nature of addiction we must
thoughtfully entertain Jung's insights, including the existence of substantive Archetypal Shadow/Archetypal Evil, even if it is difficult and
disturbing, because it is the best map we presently have of the dynamics of addiction.

If Einstein hypothesized something new in physics we would not
dismiss it out of hand, even if it was initially very difficult to understand or accept. We would give it very careful consideration. When
Jung hypothesizes something new in psychology, because of his stat-
ure and contributions to the field we are required in fairness to give it
the same careful consideration, even if what he proposes is also difficult to comprehend or accept. The key question here is not whether
we automatically believe Einstein or Jung, but whether their map
formulations accurately reflect the phenomenon or not. Their track
records are both outstanding in their fields of study. This does not
mean they are always unquestioningly right, but that their maps are
more often accurate than not. When a better map comes along I certainly will be happy to use it, but until then Jung's map of addiction
is the best I know of.

Jung confides in Bill W. because he believes Bill is "decent and
honest," and will understand because of his experience with alcoholism and with A.A. He believes Bill W. is the right man to tell what he
believes about alcoholism, its nature, dynamics, and treatment.

Jung concludes his letter with the famous and often quoted, "You
see, 'alcohol' in Latin is *spiritus*, and you use the same word for the
highest religious experience as well as for the most depraving poison.

The helpful formula therefore is: *spiritus contra spiritum* [spirit against spirit]." In this final paragraph of his letter, Jung links transpersonal evil directly with alcoholism and addiction. The contrast between "the highest religious experience," informed by the transpersonal powers of goodness and light, and "the most depraving poison," informed by the transpersonal powers of evil and darkness, is more than suggested. The helpful formula, the antidote to the transpersonal evil aspect of addiction, is the transpersonal goodness deriving from the spiritual realm of healing and grace. It is the spirit of "the highest religious experience" that neutralizes and holds in check the spirit of the transpersonal evil of addiction. Jung is describing here the war of the gods in addiction, both vying for the hearts and souls and lives of human beings.

Aspects of this transpersonal evil, which I call Archetypal Shadow/Archetypal Evil, will be explored further in Chapter Two on the psychodynamic development of addiction and in Chapter Three, which is completely devoted to understanding Archetypal Shadow/Archetypal Evil in myth, fairy tales, and religion and in clinical literature as the unintegratable aspects of the psyche. In Chapter Four I will show how the "*spiritus contra spiritum*" is operationalized in the recovery process of the Twelve Steps of A.A.

The correspondence between Bill W. and Carl Jung is loaded with seminal ideas that have shaped and informed the A.A. program. It also holds seeds of a future understanding of alcoholism and addiction in a new way, opening the gates to mapping the true nature of addiction psychologically, by incorporating new insights from Jungian psychology and the phenomena of Archetypal Shadow/Archetypal Evil, and revealing why A.A., the Twelve Steps, and the Fellowship are the most effective approach in confronting and successfully treating alcoholism and addiction. I believe that the Bill W.-Carl Jung letters are a gold mine of previously untapped, unexplored riches with far-reaching implications for understanding the phenomena of addiction.

CHAPTER TWO

The Psychodynamics of Addiction: Development of a Typical Addiction Process

There are essentially five major stages in the development of a typical psychological addiction.

Stage 1 – The Ego/Persona identification alignment with the false self

Stage 2 – The development of the Personal Shadow

Stage 3 – The introduction of the Potentially Addictive Behavior

Stage 4 – The creation of the Addiction-Shadow-Complex

Stage 5 – The Addiction-Shadow-Complex takes over the psyche

(Please refer to the diagram "Development of the Addiction" on page 34).

STAGE 1 – THE EGO/PERSONA IDENTIFICATION ALIGNMENT WITH THE FALSE SELF

This psychodynamic model relies heavily on traditional concepts from Jungian psychology, not just because I am a Jungian analyst, but because I believe that the Jungian map has the theoretical concepts to best describe and most accurately reflect what is actually going on in the development of alcoholism and addiction. It has the capacity as a psychological system to chart and delineate the complicated and unique landscape of addiction, which is the phenomenon we are trying to understand.

What I will describe is the typical development of an addiction. It will not replicate everyone's experience, but from the feedback I've received from recovering individuals, it is reflective of the process in general in the vast majority of cases. Where people's experience differs from this theoretical model, it is more like variations on a theme than a completely different process. This is not intended in any way to be the final word on this subject.

Psychologically, the ego is the central organ of our consciousness; it is the air traffic controller of what we see and think and feel and sense, intuit, and experience. It perceives, selects, focuses, concentrates, emphasizes, organizes, and processes our relationship to ourselves, to the world, and to other people. It makes our choices and beliefs and decisions and judgments and values and gives us the green light to act or not to act. It defends its existence and integrity against threats to its power, control, and survival. We identify ourselves with our egos. The sense of "I"ness derives from our ego-complex system.

Weak egos are poorly adapted psychological organs, which find it difficult to negotiate the inner and outer worlds of reality. Weak egos may result from poor, neglected, abusive developmental foundations, from trauma, from biological or genetic problems, or from the inability to synthesize and integrate the complex circuitry necessary to create and operate a well-functioning, adaptive ego mechanism. Weak egos may also result from the effects of mental illness or physical deterioration and disease.

A strong, healthy ego serves us well and allows us to grow and develop and adapt and change in response to life's demands. Without a healthy, strong ego complex at the center of our consciousness, we cannot explore or relate adequately to the contents of the unconscious.

Most people initially identify their egos with their personas. The persona is the mask we wear in relation to the world and others. It is created through a combination of socialization, societal expectations, one's experience of the world, and the natural attributes and tendencies of the individual. It combines elements of how we want to see ourselves, ideally, and how we want the world to see us, as well as how the world does see us and wants us to be. Our persona defines our social identity; it is constructed in relation to the roles we play in our lives and in our world, how we want to look and be seen. It is the face we wear to be presentable and acceptable to our society. It is not necessarily who we really are, but who we want and pretend to be to others and, many times, to ourselves. The great danger of an ego over-identification with the persona is that we begin to believe that we *are* our well-constructed, overly idealized mask, and not who and what we really are, warts and all.

Personas are not inherently bad; they are very important, and necessary for us to function in the world, to work, to play, and to interact with others. People without enough persona are deficient in their ability to deal with the real world. They never seem to know what to say or how to act, and are always getting in trouble and upsetting other people because they have developed no sense of what is or is not appropriate in different social and relational situations. They are often experienced by others as tactless, rude, annoying, offensive, and "not having a clue" about how to behave in public.

The problem in individuals who develop an addiction is usually not one of little or no persona, but too much—too thick, too heavy a persona. When the ego identifies with the persona and not with the true Self, Jungians call this an alignment identification with a false self. It would be like someone falling in love with a puppet he or she has created, somehow believing it to be a real human being capable of love and relationship. When the truth is realized, a rude, painful awakening awaits. It is a self-deception where we believe in what is ultimately not the reality of who in fact we truly are. Another analogy is the difference between someone who, in the Judeo-Christian tradition, relates to the living God, Yahweh, and someone who worships an inanimate object of his or her own creation (for example, the golden calf of the Old Testament). The true Self, like Yahweh, says, "I am the lord of the psyche; thou shalt have no strange, false selves before me."

This Ego/Persona identification alignment with the false self leads directly to the Personal Shadow and to stage 2 in the development of the addiction.

STAGE 2 – THE DEVELOPMENT OF THE PERSONAL SHADOW

The personal shadow resides in that part of the psyche described in Jungian psychology as the personal unconscious, in contrast with the collective unconscious from which the impersonal, objective, uni-

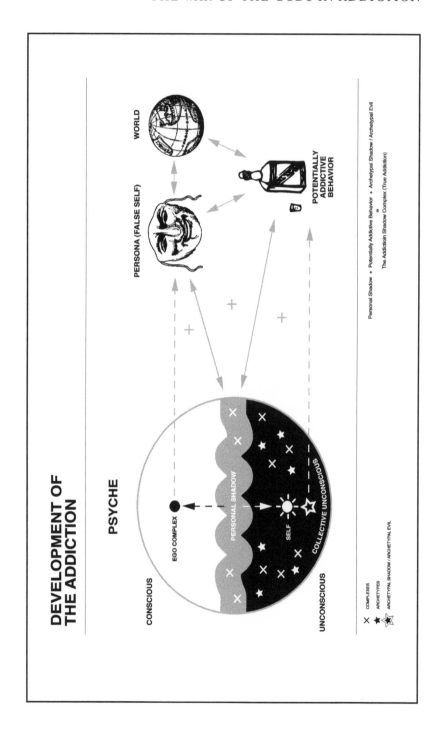

versal contents of the archetypes derive. Our personal shadow is the "hidden unconscious aspects of [ourselves], both good and bad, which the ego has either repressed or never recognized."[1] It is all of the incompatible thoughts, feelings, desires, fantasies, and actions that we have suppressed and repressed into the personal unconscious, along with our more primitive, undifferentiated impulses and instincts. In the Freudian view of the psyche, it is what Freud identifies as the whole of the "unconscious." It is what I like to describe as the personal psychological garbage can of our psyches.

Jung says of the personal shadow, "The shadow is a moral problem that challenges the whole ego-personality, for no one can become conscious of the shadow without considerable moral effort. To become conscious of it involves recognizing the dark aspects of the personality as present and real."[2]

We all have a personal psychological garbage can and we all have a personal shadow. The contents of our personal shadow are directly related to our persona. All the unacceptable, rejected aspects of who we are go into our personal shadow, where we try initially to bottle them up and suppress them, to lock them up securely hidden in the dark closets, attics, and basements of our psyches, where we hope no one will venture and discover these disowned bastard children, our personal shadows.

Of course, the more we identify with our persona, the more gets crammed into our personal shadow. It can become filled to the brim. Sometimes, to our embarrassment and shame, it begins to emit bad odors, overflow, and leak out to bother us and be noticed by others; so we try to tighten the lid, plug the leaks, or reinforce the bolted door (suppress, repress, deny, and rationalize more); or we use a sanitizer (put on the mantle of social respectability by joining the Rotary Club, the Junior League, or becoming a deacon in the church); or we try to bury it deeper in the psyche (even more denial, forgetting and avoiding, or creating greater and more elaborate precautions to hide the personal shadow from detection by others). None of these strategies is ultimately effective. The shadow will have its say and its day one way or the other.

These efforts and strategies require more and more ego defenses and psychological energy to hold the shadow at bay from consciousness. The personal shadow then begins draining prime and necessary energy from the ego-complex system. The defenses required to hold this mounting monster in check, to keep it from becoming conscious, continue to grow and deplete the ego system of the vital energy needed to adapt and function in the everyday world. In addition, psychic energy is required to keep up and maintain our personas. The greater the incongruity between our persona and who we really are, the greater the energy required to defend and maintain the system. You get the picture: more and more tension and stress are being created psychologically, more and more vigilance and defense are required on a daily basis, until it begins to become overwhelming and unbearable—more and more impossible to maintain.

The reality of the personal shadow demands to be recognized and dealt with. The screams and moans and rattling chains from our psychic closets, attics, and basements get louder and louder, harder and harder to ignore, avoid, or forget.

Of course, the demand of the personal shadow to be let out into the light of day, to be free, is completely at odds with what the persona is demanding. The conscious ego position is now caught between a rock and a hard place; it has overidentified with the persona, does not know what to do with this crude and crazy personal shadow stuff, has no acceptable place to put it, and seemingly has no alternatives in face of these completely opposite competing demands. It truly appears to be an irreconcilable no-win situation, with no way out.

This part of the process leads us to Stage 3 in the development of the addiction; this is where the potentially addictive behavior enters the scene to—seemingly—save the day, alleviate the tension and stress on the ego system, and solve the problem—or at least that's what it promises.

STAGE 3 – THE INTRODUCTION OF THE POTENTIALLY ADDICTIVE BEHAVIOR

The seemingly unresolvable tension of the persona and the personal shadow increases until the person gets physically or psychically sick. Physically, there are often the symptoms of high blood pressure, ulcers, intestinal and heart problems, etc. Psychically, symptoms often constellate around anxiety, depression, PTSD, and obsessive compulsive disorders. Neurosis and even psychosis are not unusual. To other persons it looks like exhaustion, burnout, or a nervous break-down—not being able to take it anymore.

As so often in life, necessity becomes the mother of invention. If the ego wants to avoid the pending breakdown, it has basically two choices: One, it can choose to get help medically, psychologically, or spiritually; that is, it can be aided by new grace or insight or a will-ingness to change through some form of counseling or analysis that is capable of effectively addressing the persona/personal shadow prob-lem. Two, it can seek relief through a strategy of escape and avoid-ance, through a coping mechanism that becomes concentrated around the repetitive discharging of tension provided by various potentially addictive behaviors such as use of alcohol or drugs, gambling, sex, food, work, relationships, or whatever.

There are many specific individual ways and reasons why a per-son develops his or her addiction, but the final outcome is the same. Everyone, of course, has his or her particular story. The basic pattern, though, is the same—the dynamics are very typical and predictable and follow a common course. What is fascinating about this is that almost every alcoholic or addicted person I've ever known initially believed that they were "the exception to the rule." They allowed that it might all be true for everyone else, but not for them. This is the classic denial at the core of all psychological addictions, but more importantly, it also points out an aspect of the addicted individual that operates narcissistically to separate him or her from the very people—peer alcoholics and addicts—who could truly see, under-stand, and appreciate what the suffering addicted individual is going through. Remember what Jung said in his letter to Bill W. about a person not protected from heaven, and isolated in society, how that person "cannot resist the power of evil." This very aspect of the psy-chological makeup of alcoholic and addicted individuals sets them up to become possessed by the addiction. It certainly does have a dia-bolical feel to it in an archetypal sense, in that there is a more power-ful impersonal dynamic influencing, dictating, and controlling the individual's behavior. The very thing that could help save the indi-vidual is rejected out of hand and in advance, so that one unconsciously, unknowingly condemns oneself to the path that leads to death and destruction. Obviously, a power greater than oneself is necessary for salvation.

Now that the potentially addictive behavior has entered the scene, the stakes are getting higher, and so is the danger that the behavior will become a full-fledged, completely uncontrollable addiction. At this point in the process, for many people, there is still a chance that through willpower, self-discipline, insight, therapy, or ego-control they can avoid the pitfalls of becoming addicted. Many people at this stage, in a minimizing way, describe their potentially addictive behavior as recreational, social, experimental, or normal (it may not be an addiction yet, but it certainly qualifies as a level of abuse of alcohol or drugs or whatever that is getting dangerous). It is destructive and unhealthy, but it is still under conscious ego control to possibly moderate or change. I want to reiterate that pharmacological, behavioral, and ego-insight therapies can be effective at this stage in the process, before it has developed into a full-blown addiction. This is true because it is still prior to the entrance of the aspects of Archetypal Shadow/Archetypal Evil into the dynamic of the addiction process. In general, persona, personal shadow, and repetitive bad habit issues on their own can be treated effectively with traditional therapies, including psychoanalysis.

Some people have no window of opportunity to avoid psychological addiction. For them, the very first time they engage in the potentially addictive behavior, they are hooked—they are addicted from the beginning, from the very first moment of use and onward. I know of individuals raised in alcohol-free situations who never touched alcohol until much later in life, but after the first drink, they were as hopelessly consumed by it as those who had abused alcohol for decades before they crossed over the line to addiction. Some people are biologically or hereditarily predisposed to being addicted, but even those who seem, physiologically, to be loaded time bombs for addiction still cross over and participate in the same psychological addiction dynamics that take over, kill, and destroy others who may have taken a longer road to that door. This often seems to be the case with alcohol and many Native Americans.

The activation of the potentially addictive behavior then leads us to Stage 4 in the development of the addiction. It is what I describe as the creation of the "Addiction-Shadow-Complex," where the coming together of all the necessary elements, including Archetypal Shadow/Archetypal Evil, coalesce into the insane, self-destructive, murderous phenomenon we know as a true addiction.

STAGE 4 – THE CREATION OF THE ADDICTION-SHADOW-COMPLEX

From a Jungian perspective, the potentially addictive behavior allows for a needed type of release and expression of the personal shadow in a way that the conscious ego, with its overidentification with the persona, will not allow. The Jungian analyst Linda Leonard, in her wonderful book *Witness to the Fire: Creativity and the Veil of Addiction*,[3] argues strongly that the personal shadow is looking for any way it can find to express itself, and often the addictive behavior is the first chance in many years the shadow has had to get out of the closet, the attic, or the basement, and it takes full advantage of its opportunity to take all it can get, oftentimes with a vengeance. This often manifests as the wild, dangerous, risk-taking, embarrassing, out-of-control behavior of people when they are drinking or using, which is usually so different from their normal way of acting.

Leonard sees alcoholism and other addictions as attempted short-cuts to creativity—a quick ticket, a free ride to paradise for the art-ist—but, of course, it never really works out; it is only a very tempt-ing illusion. Perhaps this is why so many artists seem to be seduced by the allure of addiction—as with Satan and his false promises. Leonard says that ultimately addiction swallows up and destroys cre-ativity. She says all addictions are killers and, as I stated earlier, that the addiction ultimately wants everything burned and sacrificed on its altar alone.

At this point in the addiction process, others often observe what is known as the Dr. Jekyll/Mr. Hyde phenomenon—the fundamen-tal personality change of the individual when they are participating in the addictive behavior, contrasting with when they are not. When they are sober and straight they can be the nicest, kindest, most lov-ing and gentle people on earth (Dr. Jekyll). When they are drinking or using, they can become the meanest, cruelest, most brutal and abusive monsters alive (Mr. Hyde). Notice the contrast between the Dr. Jekyll behavior (nice, kind, loving, gentle), which fits right in with an ego overidentification with a positively idealized persona, and the Mr. Hyde behavior (mean, cruel, brutal, abusive), which fits right into the expression of the most raw, unintegrated, repressed personal shadow. Robert Louis Stevenson, who wrote the story of Dr. Jekyll and Mr. Hyde in the late 1800s, reported that he got the idea for his novel from his own dreams, which of course would have been giving him abundant nightly feedback on his personal shadow.

The story is a perfect literary illustration of the potential outcome of an unintegratable split between the persona and the personal shadow. It even incorporates the use of drugs in the process of the story line. "The story tells of a doctor who takes a drug that changes him into a new person, physically ugly and spiritually evil. As a psychological inquiry into the nature of evil that exists in all people [personal shadow], the novel brilliantly anticipates much modern psychological fiction [and much psychological nonfiction as well]."[4]

Under the influence of the addictive behavior, the other side, the shadow, comes out in ways that are often completely the opposite of the typical normal attitudes, behavior, and personality of the individual. Shy introverts dance on tables, timid gentle souls pick fights with motorcycle gangs, morally righteous preachers consort with ladies of the evening, and conservative cautious folks become high-stakes, high-risk gamblers. In these ways, the personal shadow reinforces, encourages, and becomes dependent upon the addictive behavior to express itself, to have any existence in the light outside of the closet, the attic, and the basement where it has been locked up and hidden for so long. Often the addictive behavior allows the personal shadow the only opportunities to live and to be. The more cut off and unconscious we are of our personal shadows, the more vulnerable we are to having those shadows break out and be set free for a time by addictive behaviors.

This bond between the addictive behavior and the personal shadow results in a very powerful alignment complex in the psyche. It is more powerful than almost all other structures and complexes in the personality. This bond between the addictive behavior and the personal shadow is at least half of the ingredients necessary to create the Addiction-Shadow-Complex. It's a lot like a man up to his chin in deep water, who doesn't know how to swim—and land is very far away. He hasn't drowned yet, but it's getting pretty inevitable unless something dramatic and unexpected happens to change the scenario.

This leads to the last part of the process in creating the Addiction-Shadow-Complex, where the final crucial ingredient of Archetypal Shadow/Archetypal Evil is added, enters the dynamic, and solidifies the addiction forever.

STAGE 5 – THE ADDICTION-SHADOW-COMPLEX
TAKES OVER THE PSYCHE

The combination of the addictive behavior, the personal shadow, and Archetypal Shadow/Archetypal Evil now becomes the most dominating, formidable power in the psyche, literally taking over and displacing the normal ruling ego complex and substituting for it a creation of its own. The Addiction-Shadow-Complex soon puts the ruling ego completely out of control—deposes, displaces, and freezes it out into powerlessness. The Addiction-Shadow-Complex replaces the ruling ego complex with its own ruler, a puppet pseudo-king who serves ultimately only the desires, interests, and agendas of the addiction, which cares nothing for any other values or needs of the person, the psyche, or the true Self, or for anyone or anything else. This is the all-consuming nature of addiction.

The dynamic of this coup in the psyche is qualitatively and quantitatively different from being temporarily caught in an emotionally charged complex or in an ego overidentification with a false self. It is different from most other psychiatric disorders. In neurosis the ego continues to function, though relatively ineffectively, and in psychosis there is little or no operating ego because it has been swamped and washed out, overwhelmed by the contents of the floodwaters of the unconscious. In personality disorders, the ego continues to function and collude with unhealthy lifelong patterns and complexes established early in childhood. I suppose I am proposing a new and different category of ego functioning in relation to addiction.

In addiction, there is a permanent hijacking of the entire psychic system; the normal ego complex and all its functions are as if put under a powerful diabolical spell that suspends and paralyzes them—the whole kingdom and everything in it. The addiction then replaces the old system with an entire ruling ego system equipped to perceive, judge, and act in as skilled, adaptive, and self-serving a way as the originally functioning, normal ego complex system. Of course it is an imposter, a liar, a deceiver and charlatan, but now the addicted person, his true Self and healthy ego, are helpless and powerless to fight or even object to the new dictatorship established by the Addiction-Shadow-Complex. It's as though we fell into our deepest, darkest, most destructive and debilitating complex, which we can, normally, eventually come out of, but in this case we are stuck and trapped in it, seemingly forever—truly a nightmare scenario.

I know that this description of what happens to the normal ego system when the Addiction-Shadow-Complex takes over is highly metaphorical, mythological, and narrative in nature. It is not clinical and sequential in the way we usually expect, but here I am trying to describe a phenomenon on the edges of our ability to understand, much less to adequately describe. There are elements of mystery and power and archetypal unknowns in this process that I only have glimpses of, so I offer the best description I can for now.

What is most important to understand, in the development process of the addiction, is that in this Stage 5, the entire psyche, ego, and personality are taken over and ruled by the Addiction-Shadow-Complex. The addiction at this point completely possesses the individual person, and has taken away the normal ability of ego, willpower, self-discipline, choice, insight, and good intentions to truly have an effect or impact to any significant degree. The prime directive is now the addiction and its agendas; everything else revolves around it and is secondary to and subsumed by it. In A.A., it is described in Step One as the powerlessness and unmanageability of our lives because of alcoholism.

Let me clarify here: The Addiction-Shadow-Complex will allow a person to continue to function in seemingly normal ways, in many or even most areas, as long as those decisions and behaviors in no way challenge, threaten, or attempt to thwart the primary agenda of the addiction, which is to continue the person's participation in the addictive behavior. As in a occupied country, one can operate relatively normally in daily life and activities as long as one does nothing in any way to challenge or threaten the ruling regime—anything of that nature will result in paying a very high price and being severely punished. Resistance is a very dangerous thing. The Addiction-Shadow-Complex knows how to press all the pain and shame and obsession buttons.

Many spouses and friends of practicing alcoholics know what this feels like from the other side. They can do anything they want, except get between a practicing alcoholic and his or her bottle of booze. If they do they will be sorry, and can get seriously hurt. This is the menacing pressure family and friends get to *not* confront the reality of the addiction, but to collude in rationalization, justification, and denial, and to become enablers. In many ways it seems safer for everybody *not* to provoke the Addiction-Shadow-Complex (the Tyranno-saurus Rex in the living room).

I've been asked about how the Addiction-Shadow-Complex applies to what are called "functional alcoholics" and "binge drinkers." By "functional alcoholic," I mean a person who drinks regularly, heavily, and sometimes gets falling-down drunk, but always functions in his or her roles as parent, spouse, and worker. They don't miss work, forget to pick up the kids from practice, or ignore their mom's birthday because of their drinking. There are many varieties of alcoholic individuals in many different stages of the debilitating process. What are called "functional alcoholics" may or may not be addicted. Some like to party too much, drink too often, abuse alcohol and get drunk too frequently, but could slow down or stop if they chose to do so. According to my definition, they are not addicted. Others, whose patterns of drinking may look very similar, are actually very different. These folks do not have the ego ability and willpower to stop or control their drinking even if they want to; they are truly addicted. Some so-called "functional alcoholics" are addicted, others are not. This cannot be decided based on drinking patterns alone. You can't judge a book by its cover; you need to know the story that's going on inside. The same applies to diagnosing alcoholism and other addictions: you need to know the story of what's going on inside to figure it out.

Nonaddicted "functional alcoholics" probably have an easier road to becoming addicted "nonfunctional alcoholics" than most others. If you are playing with fire on the edge all the time, it's a lot easier to get burned and slip into the black hole. The term "functional alcoholic" tends to focus away from what is central to addiction and to confuse people into minimizing, denying, and rationalizing what addiction is; the term leads to more misunderstanding, less clarity, and just isn't very helpful.

"Binge drinkers" also may or may not be addicted. If they are addicted, then once they begin drinking they cannot stop. Some people just enjoy getting drunk periodically and could modify their drinking if they wanted to, but they don't. Of course, true alcoholics always claim they are able to control their drinking.

This whole question of the "functional alcoholic" and the "binge drinker" illustrates how central the psychological component is to understanding addiction. Too often people want to focus on behavior or biology alone, and do not want to consider psyche in the equation. I know of instances where Catholic priests and churchgoers who are recovering alcoholics have been able to receive the eucharistic wine without it triggering the Addiction-Shadow-Complex. I am not recommending that individuals put themselves at risk by trying this, but it certainly raises the question of what is going on phenomenologically. Why does this wine in communion not trigger the addiction when any other alcohol use does? The answer, I believe, is in the psychological/spiritual part of the equation. Perhaps the sacred wine is being taken and received in a completely nonaddictive way psychologically. This may not be as strange as it seems. People with food addictions tell me that they are very clear about the difference between when they are eating food for normal, healthy, nutritional reasons and when they are eating out of their Addiction-Shadow-Complex. When they are eating food for normal reasons it does not trigger the overwhelming compulsion/craving desires and activate the addiction. Most often, eating addictively is triggered by emotions, not the existence of food. This is clearly a psychological distinction not dictated by mere biological exposure to the addictive substance.

I have also worked with recovering alcoholic and drug-addicted individuals who suffer from medically legitimate chronic pain problems that require regular pain medication. This is, of course, dangerous territory for an alcoholic or drug-addicted individual, and the pain medication could easily trigger the Addiction-Shadow-Complex and out-of-control use. What I have observed and what has been reported to me a number of times is that if the person takes only exactly the amount and frequency of medication prescribed by the doctor for the legitimate medical reasons there is not a problem. If, on the other hand, the individual gives himself or herself permission to experiment, or take more of the pain medication, or take it more frequently than prescribed, it triggers the Addiction-Shadow-Complex, and out-of-control use ensues. Again, I am not encouraging alcoholic or addicted individuals to put themselves in jeopardy with pain medication. There are obviously many addicted individuals who cannot expose themselves to any pain medication without it triggering a relapse, but in the cases cited above, it is clear that the psychological factor is at least as important as the biological and behavioral exposure. The psyche plays a much bigger part in addiction than most people believe or understand.

In addiction, the potentially addictive behavior has moved from influencing and tempting and seducing the ego, its thoughts, judgments, perceptions, feelings, decisions, and actions (what would be classified in the *DSM IV* diagnostic manual as alcohol abuse or drug abuse) to taking over the whole person physically, mentally, emotionally, and spiritually (what would be classified in the *DSM IV* diagnostic manual as alcohol dependence or drug dependence), which would be a true psychological addiction, according to my criteria. It becomes more powerful than the original ego-persona identification alignment, and actually replaces it. Continuing the addictive behavior under the Addiction-Shadow-Complex is the number one priority in the psyche —more important than friends, family, marriage, career, health, and even life itself.

Marion Woodman, the well-known Jungian analyst who has written a great deal on addiction, especially regarding eating disorders in women, says that "at the core (the heart) of every addiction is an energy which ultimately wants the person's very life."⁵ Her experience with addiction leads her to the conclusion that the addiction wants everything for itself, and if that means that the individual must be destroyed in the process, that is just the way it is. She believes that an addiction truly has a spirit of evil, or put another way, there is an evil spirit in every addiction.

I cannot state strongly enough that to describe this core of addiction as a killer is not a dramatic overstatement to get your attention or an alarmist exaggeration; it is the stone-cold truth and reality of addiction. Jung's comments in his letter to Bill W. certainly support this idea, and so does the experience of millions of alcoholic and addicted individuals, their families and friends, and all the therapists and addictions counselors who have gotten into hand-to-hand mortal combat with this awesome, psychological, spiritual monster.

The final and key component—Archetypal Shadow/Archetypal Evil—necessary to create the Addiction-Shadow-Complex requires more explanation and clarification. The next chapter is completely devoted to trying to comprehend this mysterious, difficult, borderline concept of Archetypal Shadow/Archetypal Evil as an essential ingredient in the psychodynamics of addiction.

An Exploration of Archetypal Shadow/ Archetypal Evil as an Essential Ingredient in Addiction

This idea of Archetypal Shadow/Archetypal Evil is such a mysterious concept that it easily slips away like a handful of fine sand through one's fingers or gets hopelessly confused with other concepts of evil—personal, social, moral, collective, and religious— that are not helpful for our purposes. It stirs up prejudice, projection, misunderstanding, and fanaticism. It gives unintended ammunition to self-righteous religious zealots and misguided fundamentalists, and can fuel destructive sectarian ideologies. It can also be condemned and dismissed as regression to unsubstantiated, unscientific religious formulations that could undermine advancements in medicine, psychology, and sociology, turning back the clock to the murky religio-magico dark ages of explaining phenomena on the basis of faith, mythology, folk belief, and church doctrine—sounds familiar, doesn't it?

An article in the science section of the *New York Times* (February 8, 2005) stirs this very pot with the headline "For the Worst of Us, the Diagnosis may be 'Evil.'" The article raises the question of whether present mental illness diagnostic categories are adequate to address the reality of people who are serial killers, torturers, or commit repeated acts of incredible cruelty and barbarism. The article suggests that perhaps a new diagnostic category should be added—evil. Dr. Michael H. Stone argues for a hierarchy of evil, indicating the worst to the least evil range of behavior (perhaps a resurrecting of the Catholic Church's mortal sin/venial sin categories, with more gradations in between). Dr.

Robert Hare, a professor at the University of British Columbia, has already developed an instrument called the psychopathy checklist, where a point system is used to delineate the degree of evil in all of us (sounds like original sin to me!); of course, the highest scores of 30 to 40 points go to predatory killers, and most of us are a safe 5 points or below (thank God!). This is all based on supposedly sound scientific foundations.

No wonder Jung waited so long—until the end of his life—to throw out the gauntlet implicating Archetypal Evil. Some will argue that Archetypal Shadow/Archetypal Evil will only lead to even more evasion of personal psychological responsibility, as people will have one more excuse to say, "The Devil made me do it!" or that it will trigger a new wave of modern societal witch hunting (as if we don't have enough already) based on people being diagnosed as having too much Archetypal Evil in their personalities.

Trying to describe and define Archetypal Shadow/Archetypal Evil feels a lot like trying to come up with a description of God—everyone will object for one reason or another. Despite all this, I am compelled to try to make a legitimate case for the existence of Archetypal Shadow/ Archetypal Evil because it is the key to understanding the phenomenon of addiction, its unique nature, and why A.A. and the Twelve Steps are the right antidote for treating alcoholism and addiction, and why A.A. and the Twelve Steps have had success like no other treatment approach in human history.

An Overview of Concepts of Evil

There are libraries' worth of books written on the subject of evil, but the kind of evil I am trying to pin down and define is universal, archetypal, unintegratable evil, evil that cannot be transformed and metabolized and synthesized in a normal way in the psyche.

John Sanford, a Jungian analyst, has written a book titled *Evil: The Shadow Side of Reality*, where he surveys many of our major notions of evil. He begins by questioning the very existence of evil beyond the subjectivity of the individual. He says, "What is seen as good and what is seen as evil varies with the point of view of the observer, which brings up the question of whether there is an absolute viewpoint about good and evil."[1]

Sanford goes on to describe what we view as "natural" evil: disease, floods, hurricanes, earthquakes, etc., caused by the impersonal aspects of nature. He contrasts this "natural" evil with "moral" evil, involving human motives of aggression, power, destruction, greed, ambition, war, etc. These evils, he allows, are only a matter of human perspective, a point of view from a relatively egocentric position. They don't take into consideration evil from the archetypal or Self-perspective—from a transpersonal, divine perspective. He argues that "the healing of the soul is, fundamentally, a re-evaluation of good and evil, and therefore a shift from ego to Self."[2] Here there is a higher or broader or more comprehensive perspective on evil, which includes the ego and the human perspective but transcends it. In Jungian psychology, this broader perspective in the psyche of humans is described as the archetypal realm. It is directed by and organized around the archetype of the Self.

The archetype of the Self has been alluded to previously in describing the true or authentic Self in contrast to the false self or the ego-persona identification alignment. The true Self in Jungian psychology shares much, is even identical in many ways, with our concepts of the image and likeness of God within each person—of the Christ or kingdom within, of the indwelling of the Holy Spirit, of being one with the Buddha, of following the will of the Father, Allah, Yahweh, the Great Spirit, the Universe and, perhaps most importantly for the purposes of this book, the concept of the Higher Power in A.A. and in the Twelve Steps of its tradition.

A more formal definition of the archetype of the Self is that it is the archetype of wholeness. It is both the center and whole circumference of the psyche, embracing both the conscious and the unconscious; "it is the centre of the totality, just as the ego is the centre of consciousness."[3] It fuels, runs, organizes, and ultimately directs all of the psyche. It contains all of the knowledge, wisdom, healing, energy, and creativity necessary for each individual (regardless of their personal history) to grow, develop, and transform into the unique individual they are meant to be. Ultimately, it holds the key to our meaning and destiny in this world if we can discern it on our journey through life. In Jungian psychology, this is what is meant by the term individuation. It requires the cooperation of the ego in an alignment with the Self, which is the humbling and relativizing of the ego in relation to the Self mentioned earlier. The A.A. surrender of one's will and life to God or the Higher Power is precisely the same phenomenon.

In Sanford's survey, he does a nice job of summarizing the concepts of evil in different myths and religious traditions. In Egyptian myth, Set, the brother of Osiris, is the "personification of the evil desert, the bringer of darkness and drought. From him comes everything destructive and inimical to human life."[4]

In Norse myth, the god Loki personified evil, in contrast to the much beloved Baldur. "Loki embodies the principle of 'evil for itself' as a cosmic principle. Kerenyi says that Loki is 'the dark power which through the strength of its weakness and the boldness of its cowardice shapes the destiny of the world. ... His inventive brain, his ready wit and sardonic mockery weave them into a net that draws the whole world down into the abyss of death. ... Gradually through his double dealing (jokes and trickery), he prepares for the day when the enemies of life will be unleashed and when he will take the field at their head.' Kerenyi cites Gronbeck, the outstanding Danish authority on the Norse pantheon. Gronbeck says, 'Loki became almost a companion piece to the Christian Devil, but his origin made him far superior to the Father of Evil in subtlety of character 'because he was human and so extraordinarily demonic.'"[5] For Loki, evil is not a vehicle or a means to an end; it is an end in itself.

In Iranian Persian myth, Ahriman signifies "death, darkness, lies and the ills of mankind."[6] Ahriman, like the Judeo-Christian Devil, is "the prince of demons and commands a host of Doevas, evil beings devoted to trickery and falsehood, who strive along with their master to destroy the power of [the good Ahura-Mazda] and to draw mankind into evil ways."[7] In the cosmic duel, the good Ahura-Mazda will eventually win out. Ahura-Mazda is viewed as the supreme god and as the originating father of the holy and the evil spirit. This is similar in some ways to Judeo-Christian myth, where everything, including the Devil as angel, was originally created by Yahweh. Iranian Persian myth influenced Judeo-Christian myth in many ways, including the name "Beelzebub" for Satan in the New Testament, which "means 'lord of the flies' and comes from the lore about evil Ahriman who was said to have entered the world of humans in the form of a fly."[8]

Notice how in all these myths, including the Judeo-Christian tradition, there is a level of divine spiritual warfare, the war of the gods, a transcendent battle always going on that is completely out of the realm of human control or influence, but that is constantly and profoundly affecting us.

St. Augustine, in the fourth century, in a noble theological attempt to try and reconcile an all-knowing and good and omnipotent God with the existence of evil in the world, came up with his rather convoluted idea of evil as the "privatio boni," that is, evil as the deprivation or absence of good. St. Augustine tries to argue away the substantial existence of evil by saying that it simply exists because goodness does not occupy that same space in time and circumstance. This applies well to what Sanford categorizes as moral human evil, but St. Augustine's theory ignores aspects of Scripture—the Devil, Lucifer, the fallen angels, and hell—that argue for a different, less humanly subjective conclusion. St. Augustine reduces evil to the purely subjective human realm, which has influenced and encouraged many believers and nonbelievers to dismiss the existence of Satan and the Devil ever since, or at least to minimize and deny the reality of the phenomena that these mythic images represent.

St. Augustine doesn't seem to believe in Archetypal Evil, or at least doesn't appear to know what to do with it. The problem, of course, is that his map of evil does not describe well enough the whole phenomenon of evil as we know it. Many people's experience with evil posits powers and forces beyond the subjective moral shortcomings and weaknesses of human beings. Jung and others have vehemently objected to what they believe is St. Augustine's shortsighted oversimplification of evil.

In partial defense of St. Augustine's theory, I must note that it is true, as Jung described in his letter to Bill W., that when we are not surrounded by grace and the love of human community (the absence of good) we are much more likely to fall into the pitfalls of evil, human or otherwise.

In Buddhism, as I understand it, everything except love and compassion is ultimately illusion and doesn't really exist. This includes the nonexistence of evil. The focus of the constant practice of meditation is to become fully conscious of our ignorance of the illusory nature of all things (this focus also includes the alleviation of pain and suffering for all beings) and to cultivate the constant awareness and mindfulness of what is truly real, that is, love and compassion, which is the essence of the Buddha. In the West and in St. Augustine's view, I'm sure this would be what he considered "good."

The Buddhist model is very close to St. Augustine's formulation emphasizing the cultivation of goodness as the antidote to evil, in that if there is no room in us for evil, no vacuum, because we have filled ourselves, from the Christian point of view, with the love and goodness of God, then evil has no place to take root or reside in us, and in a sense does not exist for us as a personal, subjective, psychological/spiritual reality (so it is Buddhist illusion). Perhaps St. Augustine was unknowingly a closet Buddhist of the fourth century, and did accurately reflect a very important aspect of part of the phenomenon of evil.

In Greek mythology, there is no absolute evil; all the gods and goddesses are capable themselves of both good and evil in relation to human beings. This is an interesting idea—that the transpersonal forces may be quite a mixture of helpful and destructive energies for human beings. This would lead us logically to a position of respectful caution anytime we as humans encounter these forces. This is very much the sense of what Jung meant about the dangers of overidentifying with any archetype, good or bad, or any "ism" in the collective, because we don't know whether it will kill us, imprison us, compromise our psychological freedom, reduce our consciousness, or be a helpful aid on our journey to transformation. James Hillman's archetypal school of psychology emphasizes and elaborates on this view of the archetypes, primarily using the mythological maps given to us by Greek and Roman myth, where there is a pantheon of complicated and nuanced gods and goddesses representing a diversity, multiplicity, and richness of psychological factors (good, bad, and indifferent) to be dealt with, if possible, in a nondualistic, polytheistic way.

Good and evil in Hindu and Buddhist philosophy, as mentioned previously, are both considered illusions, non-realities. We must deal with them, but in the final analysis, in the ultimate scheme of things, they don't really exist as substantive realities.

In Judeo-Christian myth, evil in the universe derives from two basic sources, one divine (archetypal), and one human (moral). Divine or archetypal evil enters the universe when Lucifer and his band of angels decide to abandon God's will and plan on the cosmic (archetypal) level and establish their resistance movement and separate kingdom of evil apart from and in opposition to God. Human (moral) evil enters the world through Adam and Eve's freewill decision not to follow God's will and plan in this world. It is interesting to note that both forms of evil, human and divine, enter the universe through acts of free will by Adam and Eve and by the angels in exercising their right to freely choose to serve God or themselves. A.A. often refers to alcoholism as "free will run riot" (out of control).

Satan, Lucifer, and the Devil have a long, colorful, and varied mythological history, from cartoon characters and cute little children dressed with horns and red plastic pitchforks on Halloween to the most powerful, conscious evil spirit who rules over the ultimate center and core domain of the kingdom of evil.

For the purposes of understanding psychological addiction, I'm not interested in the meaning of the Devil in fairytales, myths, and stories as the trickster, or the lightning rod to consciousness, or the repressed shadow of Pan or Dionysus, or the straw man to help us learn what is morally right and wrong, or as the adversary, obstacle, or accuser who facilitates the processes of growth and development for human beings to find the good. These all describe legitimate psychological phenomena that must often be dealt with on our journeys, but they are not what I am looking for to describe Archetypal Shadow/Archetypal Evil. I'm looking for images and representations of the Prince of Darkness, the supernatural source of evil, the one who seeks to destroy and wreak havoc in the souls of human beings. In the Judeo-Christian Bible, it is referred to by many names: Belial, Satan, the Devil, Beelzebub, Legion, possession by evil spirits, the "enemy," and the Prince of this World. I'm seeking images and representations that can carry, describe, and reflect transpersonal aspects of this phenomenon I'm calling Archetypal Shadow/Archetypal Evil. I will go more deeply into the Devil and the archetypal expression of absolute evil in section three of this chapter, along with noting other myths and tales that reflect the transpersonal, unintegratable aspect of this psychological reality.

Jungian analyst Lionel Corbett, in his book *Psyche and the Sacred: Spirituality beyond Religion*, devotes almost fifty pages of his work to exploring the psychological question of evil. He looks at evil mostly from the human, moral, behavioral perspective, using the Holocaust and Hitler as his extreme examples to help people understand his paradigm of evil. He explores and discusses aspects of human evil psychologically, philosophically, and to some extent theologically. He mentions that Hitler was beaten daily as a child by an alcoholic father and that this may have greatly contributed to his out-of-proportion participation in such horrific evil inflicted on humanity. Corbett also cites the belief of psychoanalyst Ronald Fairbairn that "the psychotherapist is the successor to the exorcist, because in our times the casting out of inner demons is really about trying to heal the damage caused by early experiences with abusive caregivers."[9] This position does not lend support to the idea of the existence of Archetypal Shadow/Archetypal Evil as a transpersonal phenomenon. It seems to relegate all evil to a personalistic equation.

Corbett explores the many complexities of the relationship between mental illness and evil behavior. He posits an archetypal morality that exists universally in the unconscious of human beings as an innate psychological function, but discerning it and determining what is and is not authentic conscience is a very thorny proposition. For example, how do we explain the psychopathic individual who seems to have no conscience? These people appear to have "free choice but nevertheless choose evil and enjoy inflicting it on others. Professor Berel Lang, in *Act and Idea in the Nazi Genocide*, believes that evil consists not simply in knowing that what we are doing is evil, but in doing it *because* we know that it is evil."[10] Corbett suggests that the psychopathic individual is as close as we can get to "pure evil." He also asserts that, usually, one of the parents of a psychopathic individual is alcoholic. I wonder if, in the case of the psychopath, Archetypal Shadow/Archetypal Evil, perhaps through the influence of the alcoholic parent in some way, has not infected, poisoned, and taken control of the individual? The "malignant narcissism" that Corbett describes in the psychopathic individual shares some of the same territory psychologically with the untreated using alcoholic or addicted person at his or her worst (the lying, cheating, stealing, etc.). He also points to biological evidence indicating that psychopathic individuals have neurological deficits in areas of the brain dealing with emotions.

Corbett doesn't say much directly about evil in relation to alcoholism and addiction in general. He does indicate that chronic hate—

especially on a collective societal level, because it fuels and energizes people away from feeling hopeless—can "become addictive" and "take on a life of its own," greatly affecting groups and masses of people. This certainly seems to be what happens in racism, genocide, and "holy wars."

Corbett does acknowledge the positive ability of support groups, including Alcoholics Anonymous, to help people "to contain their distress" so that it doesn't have to be harmfully acted out.

On the central question of transpersonal archetypal evil, he seems to be unsure of its existence: "Although we cannot say whether or not there is objective or metaphysical evil outside of individual behavior, it is clear that there are psychological processes that make people do evil things, and such behavior can be influenced by psychotherapeutic intervention."[11] This statement appears to say that evil can only be discerned on the personal subjective level of human behavior, but then he posits possible external "psychological processes that make people do evil things." He does not clarify exactly what these "psychological processes" are, but the statement suggests transpersonal forces controlling human behavior toward evil. Is he alluding to some form of Archetypal Shadow/Archetypal Evil here? It is not clear.

In Corbett's section on the dark side of the self, he indicates that "Jung believed that the power of evil is more than simply human ... that occurrences such as the Holocaust or the bombing of Hiroshima ... [were] of such magnitude ... [that they] are far too terrible to be of purely human origin. We cannot afford to have a concept of evil that is too small."[12] Now he seems to argue, along with Jung, for an archetypal nature of evil that is beyond the subjective individual. He makes no assertions one way or the other about the transpersonal or metaphysical realities of God or Satan outside of the human psyche. He takes the traditional party line that metaphysical assertions are appropriate for faith and theology and not for psychology, but that the archetypal image manifestations of those potentially metaphysical assertions in the psyche are appropriate for psychology to address and to try to understand.

According to my reading of Corbett, after some hedging and ambivalence he comes down on the side of seeing Archetypal Shadow/Archetypal Evil as substantively existing and affecting humans, and he places it psychodynamically under the Self as its archetypal shadow dark side. He see its manifestation as radical evil imaged in the Christian myth as the Antichrist. Even with such a powerful assertion, he sees this dark side, this archetypal shadow material in the psyche, as somehow much more integratable and transformable than I do. I believe the best we can do is to neutralize Archetypal Shadow/Archetypal Evil to keep it from destroying us.

On the last page of his section on evil, Corbett complicates his position even more by stating: "Sometimes, however, we come across evil that can neither be redeemed nor be contained, a force represented in folklore and mythology as a vampire or the Medusa; the only way to deal with such evil is to destroy it."[13]

He doesn't tell us exactly what this irredeemable archetypal evil is, psychologically, and doesn't distinguish it from the archetypal evil that he indicated previously *can* be redeemed and integrated. I do not agree that we, as humans, can "destroy" Archetypal Shadow/Archetypal Evil. I do not know how it can be done, and Corbett doesn't tell us. I also cannot agree with him that this evil cannot be "contained"; in fact it is my very argument that Archetypal Shadow/Archetypal Evil *is* contained by its being neutralized by the Higher Power in the first three steps of A.A.

Perhaps Corbett might argue that it is the positive light side of the Self archetype that ultimately destroys, neutralizes, or redeems the negative dark side of the Self, in Jungian terms. These ideas are very difficult for many people to comprehend. I don't disagree with this idea theoretically, but the value of such a statement to me must be when it is operationalized in psychological phenomena we can observe and verify. If the positive light side of the Self is what we see operating in the miraculous manifestation of the Higher Power in A.A. in getting and keeping people sober, and the negative dark side of the Self is the Archetypal Shadow/Archetypal Evil aspect found in the Addiction-Shadow-Complex that is neutralized and contained by the Higher Power principle in A.A., then I'm on board. If theoretical concepts cannot be brought back to the maps of actual, operationalized psychological phenomena that help us understand what is going on, then they are of very little value.

I believe that Corbett, in general, supports the idea of the existence of Archetypal Shadow/Archetypal Evil, though we may disagree on some aspects of its nature, dynamics, and manifestations. I applaud his heroic efforts to even attempt to wrestle with the question of evil in all its forms. It is a complicated, difficult, and probably impossible task, yet it needs to be tackled, studied, and discussed in the best way we can. The phenomenon of evil, especially of Archetypal Evil, is too important and too powerful for us not to try to explore and understand it. Too much depends on what we find.

Scott Peck, the well-known author and psychiatrist, wrote a book titled *People of the Lie: The Hope for Healing Human Evil*, where he explores the idea of evil.[14] He focuses on human evil, bad people, and moral questions in general. He talks about how human beings use their free will to choose and align and immerse themselves with, and then ultimately become, evil. He goes on to acknowledge a form of transpersonal evil that he sees as Satanic possession, as contrasted with misdiagnosed psychiatric disorders. Peck originally did not believe in the reality of the Devil or evil spirits, but after witnessing two spirit possessions and participating in two exorcisms, he now does believe they are actual and real phenomena.

He posits a range of spiritual possessions, moving from less powerful evil spirits all the way up the line to the big number one, Satan. Peck believes possession involves fixations at certain ages and stages of development when people stopped growing and developing in a normal, healthy way. Peck does not do a good job here of distinguishing this from the more common mental/emotional disorders traced back to early development in childhood or to other stages of life transition. Peck's theory, however, does echo the belief and experience of many alcoholic and drug-addicted individuals that normal growth and development was arrested at the age and stage of development at which they began their involvement with their addictive behaviors. Peck relates that he and the exorcism teams in both of the exorcisms he witnessed "were convinced they were ... in the presence of something absolutely alien and inhuman."[15] As others who have dealt with Satanic possession have found, the evil spirit in Satanic possession, as in a true addiction, ultimately wants only death, destruction, suicide, murder, and chaos. I cite Peck's observations because I think he is picking up on Archetypal Shadow/Archetypal Evil in ways that parallel the dynamics in alcoholism and addiction.

My own experience with alcoholic and addicted individuals is that I could in many cases sense intuitively, from the moment they walked into my office, whether they were still clean and sober or whether they had begun, or were just about to begin, using again, slipping back into their addictive behavior and its insanity. Their very physical presence was palpably different from when they were committed to sobriety and not using. Psychologically they were more self-absorbed, aggressive, cocksure, grandiose, and defensive, and overall much less humble, open, and receptive. My question here is whether or not we can sometimes sense Archetypal Shadow/Archetypal Evil within an addiction when someone has succumbed once again to the influence of its psychological possession.

Peck also believes that the exorcism team operated to bring the possessed person out of their lonely isolation with the evil spirit into a supportive, loving community of goodness. Peck says, "The team gave the patients their very first experience of a true community."[16] For many alcoholics, often their first experience of a true community comes when they walk through the doors into an A.A meeting, when suddenly, unexpectedly, they are truly seen, accepted, and understood as they are.

Is the "evil spirit" underlying Satanic possession the same phenomenon as the Archetypal Shadow/Archetypal Evil underlying addiction? Are they a different manifestation of the same phenomenon? I'm not sure, but I do know that from everything I know of Satanic possession, it too, like addiction, wants everything and all of life sacrificed on its altar alone. It cares nothing if it results in death, suicide, murder, chaos, or the loss of one's soul. It appears to participate in the same killer energy found in addiction.

Harry Wilmer, Jungian analyst, mentor, friend, and founder of the Institute for the Humanities at Salado in Texas, held a symposium on "Facing Evil" in 1987. He invited speakers from around the world, from the widest range of perspectives and backgrounds, to address the subject of evil. The contents of the symposium were compiled into a book, *Facing Evil: Confronting the Dreadful Power behind Genocide, Terrorism, and Cruelty*; it is well worth reading. Several sections of the book addressed the subject of transpersonal, unintegratable evil. In Wilmer's introduction, he says, "There is a deeper evil, which is neither personal nor organizational. It is absolute Evil. This is conceptualized as the archetype of Evil. There is nothing that we as individuals can do to eradicate absolute Evil."[17] This is a profound and far-reaching assertion. It is disturbing and incredibly discouraging, as well as almost incomprehensible, to believe such powers and forces of evil exist and cannot be eliminated by human beings.

It is this aspect of addiction I am discussing and trying to understand. The poet laureate Maya Angelou poses a question that goes to the heart of the issue of Archetypal Shadow/Archetypal Evil. She asks, "Do Good and Evil exist as powers in some dimension which we cannot imagine? Are those two forces engaged in a struggle older than the stars?"[18] She alludes to an eternal, transpersonal conflict of good and evil not caused by humans, another allusion to a type of war of the gods. Is this part of what is going on in addiction? I believe so.

Scott Peck says that "Evil is in opposition to life. It is that which opposes the life force. It has ... to do with killing."[19] He views evil as the opposite of good, which, he believes, promotes life and liveliness. He says, "Evil has nothing to do with natural death; it is concerned only with unnatural death, with murder of the body or the spirit."[20] Peck emphasizes the inherent unnatural, murdering aspect of evil that many others have also noted as one of the core characteristics in alcoholism and addiction, which seems to almost gleefully destroy and murder everything it can about the natural life and goodness and health of the addicted individual.

Jesus reiterates this idea in John 8:44, that Satan was a murderer from the beginning. I believe Jung understood this about alcoholism and addiction when in his letter to Bill W. he refers to "the evil principle prevailing in this world," which is transpersonal and enters through the vulnerability caused by alcohol or other potentially addictive substances and behaviors to take complete control over the individual "who cannot resist the power of evil," which Jung boldly and directly calls "the Devil." Here Jung, by implication, clearly links addiction, the irresistibility of transpersonal evil, and the Devil in the dynamics of alcoholism.

Carl Kerenyi, the great mythologist, makes reference in James Hillman's book *Evil*, in the Studies in Jungian Thought Series, to an "archetype of evil" that he believes operates everywhere at all times. He says, like Peck, that "Evil is the act which arbitrarily disturbs the natural relationship between the two realms (of god and men) and prematurely conjures up the realm of death for a mortal being."[21] This definition of evil certainly well describes the premature, unnatural destruction and death of many alcoholics and addicted individuals. Kerenyi goes on to say that "Evil consists in the conjuring up of death."[22]

Jeffrey Burton Russell, who wrote a four-volume study on the history of the concept of the Devil, says, "Evil is meaningless, senseless destruction. Evil destroys and does not build; it rips and it does not mend; it cuts and it does not bind. It strives always and everywhere to annihilate, to turn to nothing. To take all being and render it nothing is the heart of evil. Or, as Erich Fromm puts it, evil is 'life turning against itself.'"[23]

I had a client once, a very shy, introverted young man in college, who had become overidentified with spiritual issues; he had thoughts about becoming a priest, but felt unworthy because of the temptations of the world and of the flesh, by which he was of course both attracted and repelled. He started thinking that the Devil was literally taking over his body and mind, and he imagined he was starting to grow horns out of his head. I worked with him for several months on self-acceptance of his humanness, of his sexuality, and of his imperfectness. He made progress and then had a dream where the Devil and God are going to have the final archetypal showdown, to settle once and for all this question of good and evil. The shoot-out is to take place in the golden-domed cathedral in St. Louis. My client and others are in the cathedral as the battle begins. He and some others quickly realize that they will be killed if they stay and try to watch the titanic struggle. He and some of the others leave the church guided by a kind but imperfect good woman, who is divorced. As he is being led away, he looks back and can see massive lightning and nuclear-like explosions going off and flashing from inside the dome of the cathedral, and he knows that any human who refused to leave and stubbornly stayed where they shouldn't be would be vaporized and destroyed in the great battle between God and the Devil. It was not their place for humans to witness these things.

We talked about his dream; it was perhaps the biggest, most important dream of his life. What he realized from the dream was that there were archetypal spiritual forces and energies that could not be mediated or witnessed or integrated or even contained by human beings; they needed to be left alone to be decided by the gods, they were not the realm into which humans should inject themselves, and if they did and they tried to stay and didn't get out of the way, they would be obliterated. His willingness to follow the good, yet imperfect woman in the dream was the right path to take to be saved, to not be destroyed by the archetypal energy of this spiritual warfare, which was way out of his or any other mortal's league. The dream was telling him to follow the imperfect feminine principle of Eros and relatedness, and to get out of the way and let the immortals, not humans, decide this ultimate question of good and evil.

Though my client was not addicted to anything I know of, his dream strongly asserts that there are transpersonal energies much bigger than human beings, whose conflicts cannot be arbitrated, mediated, integrated, or even witnessed by humans. This is part of what I believe occurs in the psychodynamics of addiction where Archetypal Shadow/Archetypal Evil winds up struggling and at war with Archetypal Good. Jung pointed to the archetypal healing formula in alcoholism in his letter to Bill W.: "*spiritus contra spiritum*," the great Spirit of Life against the great Spirit of Death, and none of it can be influenced or controlled by the conscious human ego. Humans basically get caught in the crossfire between these absolute archetypal forces and powers.

Maya Angelou sums up this idea better, as most poets do: "If Evil, as I suspect, is a torrential force separate from mankind and Good is a torrential force separate from mankind, then with or without our presence that terrible turmoil will continue on the cosmic level."[24]

CLINICAL AND THEORETICAL FORMULATIONS OF UNINTEGRATABLE ASPECTS OF THE PSYCHE

Let us now turn our searchlight regarding this phenomenon of Archetypal Shadow/Archetypal Evil onto the realm of existing clinical and theoretical psychodynamic formulations positing the idea of unintegratable aspects of the psyche in general.

Sigmund Freud, in his mostly ignored formulation of Eros and Thanatos, posits a core life instinct, Eros, pitted against a core death instinct, Thanatos. Freud viewed Thanatos as a death wish in each of us—a universal, impersonal, inherently self-destructive desire in all human beings; an alien part of our nature that wants to destroy us. This certainly describes many of the same attributes found in the concept of Archetypal Shadow/Archetypal Evil operating in alcoholism and other addictions.

This Eros and Thanatos theory of Freud's that we humans are constantly harboring both a life instinct and a death wish, which are transpersonal and universal, has many implications. Recent research, for example, has found that over 90% of people have had suicidal thoughts of some kind, at some time in their lives. This means that the thought of or desire to end one's life by suicide is not really a deviant or abnormal phenomenon, but is somehow a regular part of human nature. Most people struggle at one time or another in their lives with the question of whether or not life, for them, is still worth living. The great existential question of life and death—to be or not to be—seems to be a hardwired part of being human. The idea of a universal death wish seems strange at first glance, until we reflect on it as a phenomenon that challenges an overly idealized, positivistic attitude that everything is instinctively directed toward life, health, and happiness. People with addictions struggle every day against the irrational, illogical actuality that they continue to destroy themselves in spite of all the information, education, and reasonable, logical, rational arguments otherwise.

On a lower level of Thanatos, we can see how addicted and nonaddicted individuals often participate in self-sabotaging and self-destructive behaviors as they unconsciously "shoot themselves in the foot"; "leave the back door open"; keep stepping into the same hole, the same "blind spot"; or keep forgetting what should never be forgotten. The "Achilles heel" is a constant reminder of the human vulnerability in all of us, which can lead to our demise. It is fascinating to consider that there is a built-in part of all of us that wants to destroy us. Freud was definitely onto something very dark, dangerous, and frightening in his concept of Thanatos. No wonder most people would prefer it to remain in the forgotten back files of his work.

Donald Kalsched, a Jungian analyst from New York, presented a paper in Pittsburgh in October 1993 at the fall meeting of the Inter-Regional Society of Jungian Analysts entitled, "Addiction to the Lesser Coniunctio." In alchemical language, the "Lesser Coniunctio" was the term used to describe elements, substances, and chemicals that were not integratable, that could not be transformed, transmuted, changed, or united in the alchemical laboratory process. These elements must be kept from contaminating and destroying the process and thrown out or else they will ruin the rest of the work. What Kalsched is hypothesizing is that there are forces in the psyche that are inherently evil—not necessarily in a moral sense, but in a psychological sense. They are psychologically incompatible with human beings; forces inherently evil and poisonous to humans that are unintegratable and untransformable in the alchemical laboratory of the psyche. These elements and forces are diabolical in the psyches of human beings. The term *diabolical*, which we associate with the Devil and evil, literally means, "to tear apart," in contrast to the word *symbolic*, which literally means, "to put together."

Kalsched believes these forces of what he calls the "Lesser Coniunctio" can tear apart and destroy the human being. He also believes, as I do, that there is an aspect in a true addiction that is one of these diabolically destructive forces, which cannot be metabolized and integrated psychologically.

Kalsched went in another direction with his work. He zeroed in on this unintegratable aspect of the psyche in trauma victims in his groundbreaking book, *The Inner World of Trauma: Archetypal Defenses of the Personal Spirit.*[25] He theorizes a Protector/Persecutor aspect of the psyche, which is the psyche's self-portrait of its own archaic defense operations. He describes this Protector/Persecutor as not being educable, which is another way of saying it cannot be modified, integrated, or transformed by the psyche. He describes the dynamics of the Protector/Persecutor in this way: "As much as he or she [the trauma victim] wants to change, as hard as he or she tries to improve life or relationships, something more powerful than the ego continually undermines progress and destroys hope. It is as though the persecutory inner world somehow finds the outer mirror in repeated self-defeating reenactments—almost as if the individual were possessed by some diabolical power or pursued by a malignant fate."[26]

What Kalsched describes here could equally apply to the experience in most addictions—just substitute alcoholic or addicted individual for the trauma victim and the quote reads equally true for both groups of suffering souls. Though the repetitive, self-destructive, self-defeating reenactment behavior occurs in both the trauma victims and in addicted individuals, I don't believe the dynamics are completely the same. Of course, there are many people who are both trauma victims as well as addicted individuals. No single diagnosis precludes other diagnoses for many other possible psychosocial/emotional disorders. These other variables complicate and create more difficulties in the healing or recovery process, but they don't change the fundamental psychodynamics of the addiction. For example, at almost any A.A. meeting you can find alcoholics and addicted individuals who also suffer from clinical depression, OCD, anxiety, PTSD, schizophrenia, manic-depression, attention deficit disorder, etc. These disorders do not explain addiction, nor does treating them result in the effective treatment of the alcoholism or of the addiction.

In trauma victims, my observation is that the Protector/Persecutor defense complex comes and goes as needed, depending on the circumstances and the potential degree of threat to the self. In a true addiction, once the Addiction-Shadow-Complex has been activated, it takes over the psyche of the alcoholic or addicted individual. He or she cannot return to his or her more normal, functioning ego complex because it has been paralyzed and completely—not partially—overthrown by the addiction, which is then in total control physically, emotionally, psychologically, socially, and spiritually. The addiction may allow what looks like a pseudo-ego-normalcy for a time, but this is only allowed to the extent that it does not threaten or challenge the addiction agenda. It is ultimately only a pacifying, manipulative ploy designed to maintain control and domination. Inconsequential behaviors are allowed as long as they don't create a problem for the addiction. One of the biggest problems in recovery is the illusion of control the alcoholic or addicted individual has, while the Addiction-Shadow-Complex actually continues to call the shots.

Another perspective on unintegratable aspects of the psyche comes from Jungian analyst Adolf Guggenbühl-Craig, in his book *The Emptied Soul: On the Nature of the Psychopath*.[27] Guggenbühl-Craig argues that there are holes or lacunae in our psyches, which result in our becoming, in a sense, psychological invalids with no possibility or ultimate capacity for healing, growing, integrating, or getting better. In some psychological areas we are like physically handicapped, crippled individuals with perpetually limited capacities and options—what could be considered a permanent disability of the psyche. Our potentials will never achieve or return to what would be considered normal or healthy. Cure or achievement of optimal health and functioning are not possible. We all must learn to live with our limitations both physically and psychologically as aging, disease, and diminishment take their toll. If we insist on having expectations psychologically, as well as physically, that are exaggerated, unrealistic, or impossible, we just set up constant frustration, failure, disappointment, and despair.

Guggenbühl-Craig continues his line of reasoning, arguing that the psychopath is an invalid whose chronic, un-healable deficiency is a perpetual lack of Eros—that is, an innate inability to truly relate to others, to empathize or feel compassion for them—and there is nothing we or they can do about it. This is a pretty grim and hopeless scenario he proposes.

For our purposes, Guggenbühl-Craig points out and delineates another theoretical perspective supporting the existence of unintegratable aspects of the psyche. They are aspects absent or missing from the beginning, or which were somehow lost forever along the way. His theory is both interesting and fascinating to consider. It certainly presents a different perspective regarding the self-actualizing models swamping the psychological landscape of today.

There are also physiological conditions predisposing individuals towards addiction or accompanying the addiction, such as heredity, body type, physical disease, trauma, and the organic deterioration stages of alcoholism and many other addictions. These have to do with biologically unintegratable or un-healable structures and processes that cripple brain chemistry, organ functions, and the whole nervous system, as well as an individual's entire metabolic and nutritional functioning. These physiological phenomena may be mirroring and registering biologically what is going on psychologically with unintegratable aspects of Archetypal Shadow/Archetypal Evil in an addiction.

Marie-Louise von Franz, a brilliant Jungian analyst and perhaps the world's foremost authority on fairy tales, who knew Carl Jung personally, comments on this type of physical/psychological phenomenon. She says there are indications that physical and psychic energy may be but two aspects of one and the same underlying reality. "If this turns out to be the case then the world of matter will appear as, so to speak, a mirror-image of the world of spirit or of the psyche, and vice versa."[28] Jung's position on this is very clear when he says "there is no difference in principal between organic and psychic formations."[29]

Von Franz makes her own case for unintegratable aspects of the psyche when she talks about images in myth, fairy tales, and alchemy that point to bits "of inassimilable evil in the psyche which resist sublimation and which must be thrown out."[30] She also is positing the existence of psychic material that is transpersonal evil, which cannot be integrated, digested, or incorporated by the psyche and must be consciously rejected.

Von Franz continues her argument, "One alchemist observed that in the 'prima materia' (original matter) there is a certain intractable amount of 'terra damnata' (accursed earth) that defies all efforts at transformation and must be rejected. [This is very similar to Kalsched's previous reference to the "Lesser Coniunctio."] Not all dark impulses lend themselves to redemption; certain ones, soaked in evil, cannot be allowed to break loose and must be severely repressed. What is against nature, against the instincts, has to be stopped by main force and eradicated. The expression 'assimilation of the shadow' (personal shadow) is meant to apply to childish, primitive, undeveloped sides of one's nature, depicted in the image of the child or the dog or the stranger. But there are deadly germs that can destroy the human being and must be resisted, and their presence means that one must be hard from time to time and not accept everything that comes up from the unconscious."[31]

Jung himself addresses this question of integrating personal shadow versus integrating Archetypal Shadow/Archetypal Evil when he says that "it is quite within the bounds of possibility for a man to recognize the relative evil of his nature, but it is a rare and shattering experience for him to gaze into the face of absolute evil."[32]

The implications of what Jung and von Franz are saying are profound and disturbing. They point to this phenomenon, but give us no examples of these "dark impulses" which "must be resisted." What is this absolute evil? What are these "deadly germs" that can shatter and destroy the human being? Where do we see them clinically, psychologically, and in society? How do we discriminate between what is and is not assimilable in the psyche? What images and experiences are frightening and terrifying, yet integratable and necessary for our transformation, and what images and experiences "soaked in evil" will kill us if we dare to touch them? How are we to know? Do torturers, pedophiles, and psychopathic serial killers have this Archetypal Shadow/Archetypal Evil dominating and controlling their psyches? I don't know for sure.

Carl Jung, in his letter to Bill W., goes on record with his view that alcoholism—and other addictions, by extrapolation—carry this element of transpersonal evil "which is called very aptly the Devil." Von Franz is also alluding to the same Archetypal Shadow/Archetypal Evil I am talking about in addiction.

Clarissa Pinkola Estés, the Jungian analyst who wrote the very popular *Women Who Run with the Wolves*, also acknowledges that there is a type of manifest evil that does exist and is truly irredeemable.[33]

These examples from Freud, Kalsched, Guggenbühl-Craig, von Franz, and Jung are existing clinical and theoretical formulations supporting the idea that there are unintegratable aspects of the psyche already being talked about psychodynamically. I am not inventing this idea. I am hoping to add to the discussion that there are unintegratable aspects of the psyche in alcoholism and addiction, which I am calling Archetypal Shadow/Archetypal Evil, and which Jung was alluding to in his letter to Bill W.

IMAGES OF ADDICTION AND ARCHETYPAL SHADOW/ARCHETYPAL EVIL IN FAIRY TALES, MYTH, AND RELIGION

When we look to find the images of addiction and Archetypal Shadow/Archetypal Evil mirrored in fairy tales, myth, and religion, we can get a glimpse of how they operate in the psyche through the stories and characters who embody them and the ways one should respond to them.

Von Franz, for example, believed that the figure of Bluebeard represented one form of this untransformable evil. She says: "Bluebeard is a murderer and nothing more, he cannot transform his wives or be transformed himself. He embodies the death-like ferocious aspects of the animus [the psychological masculine principle, positive and negative, in a woman] in his most diabolical form; from him only flight is possible."[34]

The vampire in many legends is another example of an untransformable figure like Bluebeard, as well as an example of both

Archetypal Shadow/Archetypal Evil and addiction. The vampire is the murderer who preys on the innocent, lures and seduces them with his charms until he can sink his teeth into their necks and suck the very life blood from their veins, drop by drop, until they are too weak and drained to resist, and then they too join the ranks of the living dead. Sometimes alcoholics and drug addicts, at their worst, do look and walk around like zombies of the living dead—drained of all their blood by the vampire addiction.

You don't negotiate with a vampire. Linda Leonard says that for an alcoholic "to take the first drink is like offering his neck to Dracula—it is insanity."[35] You don't make deals with the vampire; you don't accommodate a compromise. You run for your life. You hold up crucifixes and surround yourself with the consecrated hosts of the Eucharist. You wear garlic and pray like hell every prayer you know. Metaphorically, the response to any addiction should be the same. A.A.'s way of saying this is "Whatever it takes" (to get and stay sober) is what you do.

The vampire, like addiction, wants your very life sacrificed to its agenda. The vampire and addiction live off the lifeblood of human beings. They will both kill you if they can.

Leonard, in her exceptional book, *Witness to the Fire: Creativity and the Veil of Addiction*, describes this same aspect of addiction as "The Killer"—which is above all laws, beyond all boundaries, exempt from the human condition. She says, as does Marion Woodman, both experts in working with addicted individuals, that all addictions are killers.

Kerenyi, the great mythologist mentioned previously, sees Iago from Shakespeare's *Othello* as the personification of Archetypal Evil, as the eternal human mythological figure of evil. Kerenyi quotes from Carl J. Burckhardt: "Iago is sustained and determined by the cosmic power of envy, wherever he appears, he creates doubt and despair is his harvest. He is the genius of malevolence."[36] Kerenyi says, "Iago is at work everywhere at all times."[37] Certainly in addiction there seem to be universal elements, on a recurring basis, of envy, doubt, and despair on the part of addicted individuals as well as their spouses, families, and friends.

In their book *Witches, Ogres, and the Devil's Daughter: Encounters with Evil in Fairy Tales*, Mario Jacoby, Verena Kast, and Ingrid Riedel argue that "Real Evil" in a fairy tale, as opposed to evil that is more personal and capable of modification and development, "would mean that a destructive power was at work that could not be dealt with, only avoided. Flight is the only possibility here [for alcoholics, that means don't drink!] even at the price of the hero or heroine returning ostensibly untransformed."[38]

Their advice continues, "If evil is too strong, one can only flee. Here it seems essential to keep to oneself and avoid any major rapprochement with evil [for alcoholics, this means don't sit in barrooms hoping you won't drink or don't test yourself with one drink to see if you are strong enough to handle it]. To try to integrate [this kind] of [archetypal] evil in such a situation, as in [personal] shadow integration, would lead to catastrophe."[39] Jacoby, Kast, and Riedel very much echo von Franz's position stated earlier, but once again they don't tell us just what this "Real Evil" is and what it looks like. They don't tell us where we can find it.

Von Franz, in her article "The Problem with Evil in Fairy Tales," even champions avoiding and staying away from Archetypal Shadow/ Archetypal Evil as heroic. She says, "It can be an heroic achievement to run from the power of evil, to avoid being 'possessed' by it in the literal sense."[40]

Von Franz continues, "Evil has its divine depths, into which it is irreverent to look. The mentally ill often show an unseemly lack of this respect for the divine powers, especially those of the dark side, and this lack of 'religio' may be, in part, responsible for their mental derangement. ... It would seem more normal and appropriate for men to fear the principle of evil. ... Fear of ... archetypal destructive contents in the psyche is not cowardice, but a sign of maturity."[41]

Perhaps we should expand the saying from Scripture that "the fear of the Lord is the beginning of wisdom" to include "the beginning of wisdom is also the fear of Archetypal Shadow/Archetypal Evil in any form." To avoid a black hole is not foolish or naive. To venture knowingly into its force field would be suicide. The black hole swallows up, sucks up everything—matter, gravity, even light. Nothing, it seems, can escape its powerful tractor-like beam into the dark vortex. Is the black hole another image of alcoholism and addiction, of Archetypal Shadow/Archetypal Evil that will destroy us if we get too close, suck us in and then swallow us whole? If so, we should try and stay away from the edges—the temptations, the habits, and the attitudes that put us in danger and at risk of becoming its victims. What am I talking about? If you are abusing alcohol or drugs or gambling or sex or food, stop. Stop right now, this minute, today. If you can't, you are already in the black hole of addiction. Don't use alcohol or drugs or any potentially addictive behavior "to cope with living," to mediate emotional pain, to deal with stress or escape from responsibility. Find healthier ways "to cope with living"—to deal with emotions, manage stress, and handle responsibility. Get help—join a support group, see a therapist, exercise, keep a journal, garden, talk to someone, hit a punching bag, take a vacation, let yourself cry, write a letter, create something, delegate, change jobs, pray, meditate, do Tai Chi, go on a retreat, volunteer, play, etc.

Don't get into habit patterns that can too easily become dependency. Don't drink alcohol every day; it takes the last drop of alcohol 48 hours to completely metabolize out of your body. If you drink every day, your body, your psyche, your whole system, is never alcohol-free. My personal policy is to never have a drink when I "need" one. On the days I come home so stressed out and exhausted that I say to myself, like so many other people, "Boy, I sure could use a drink today!"— that's the one day I make sure I don't have a drink. I'm trying to avoid using alcohol to self-medicate, to escape, "to cope with living" my life. I'm trying not to put myself foolishly on the edge of the black hole.

There is a Grimm's fairy tale, "Clever Gretel," which images many of the core elements and attitudes of a person in an alcoholism addiction process. Gretel is a cook, a servant; she wears shoes with red heels and with them on she feels very pretty. She comes home and celebrates her good feeling with a drink of wine. The wine makes her hungry, so she tastes the best of whatever she is cooking for the master and justifies herself that the cook must know what the food is like (rationalization and self-permission thinly disguised behind her professed motives).

One day, the master of the house asks her to cook a special meal because guests are coming. She roasts two birds for the occasion. When they are ready, the guests have not yet arrived (temptation enters). The master goes off to fetch the guests, and while he is gone, she starts drinking again, essentially gets drunk, and eats up all the dinner by herself, rationalizing, excusing, and justifying her presumptuous, self-indulgent behavior the entire time. When the master returns with the guests, Clever Gretel has to think fast to get out of this one, so she tells the guests that the master plans to cut off their ears. With this news, the guests run away terrified. Gretel then screams, goes to the master, and tells him the guests have run off and stolen his roasted chickens. The master gets so angry and upset with this news, he grabs the carving knife and runs after the guests, who think he is going to cut their ears off, and so the guests run away even faster than before. And so, the slapstick tale worthy of the Three Stooges ends.

The tale is amusing on one level, as a trickster story—seeing how Clever Gretel will escape from a seemingly impossible situation—but what is more fascinating to me is how in this tale many of the typical psychological elements are at play, mirroring the process development of the alcoholism/addiction dynamic.

Gretel is a servant, a cook, but she operates on a psychologically inflated, grandiose basis, as if she were the master of the house. So often in alcoholism and addiction the grandiosity and inflation is a compensation for low self-esteem and feelings of inferiority. Gretel's rationalizations, excuses, and self-justifications are all revolving around a basic core of narcissistic entitlement, defended by the classic denial dynamic of alcoholism and addiction. Her red heels are hot and haughty and provide an external source of value and self-esteem; she feels pretty when she wears them. The shoes also reflect a stilted, elevated, inflated self-image/persona, which is not well grounded. Her vanity is her initial excuse to steal the master's wine and best food.

In this story, you can see the direct connection between Gretel's identification alignment with the persona false self, and the potentially addictive behavior in the alcohol and food, which leads to an ever-expanding, voracious hunger and self-deception that quickly becomes all-consuming and out of control. Her self-permission knows no bounds, as she goes from tasting the master's best food to eating it all up. She goes from a celebratory glass of wine to downing the whole bottle. To cover her indiscretions, she must concoct an elaborate story, as so many alcoholics and addicted folks do when they have blown it. She lies and cheats and steals and tries to make others responsible for her behavior. She operates out of constant and complete denial. She seems to have no conscience about the consequences of her behavior, as all dishonesty and deception is justified to hide her dangerous, destructive, and addictive behaviors.

Gretel doesn't have enough willpower, self-discipline, self-control, or ego ability to curb or control her insatiable impulses to eat and drink. If she is not yet addicted, she is on the edge of the cliff with the ground giving way. Where will it end? Gretel doesn't get caught this time, that we know of, but if the pattern persists and she doesn't learn, or modify her behavior, it will be just a matter of time before she hits bottom, it all catches up with her, and the game will be up.

Alcoholic and addicted individuals often tell themselves and others so many lies to cover their addiction that they begin not to be able to distinguish truth from falsehood. The line blurs between fact and fiction, and they begin to believe their own lies.

Another aspect of Gretel's tale that seems accurate for so many with alcohol and addiction problems is how truly quick and clever they are. Many are very intelligent, smart, and well educated. Addiction is not because people are stupid.

I remember the first open A.A. meeting I attended. I thought for a moment I had just stepped into a depository of all the wisest men and women philosophers in the universe. I had to keep reminding myself that this was a room full of recovering alcoholics. Some of the most convincing "bs" was from folks who knew nothing yet about recovery because they had stopped drinking the day before. That didn't seem to slow them down from going on and on as if they were experts on the subject of sobriety and had it all figured out; as if they had all the answers. (A.A. distinguishes between those who talk a good talk and those who really walk the walk.) Of course these neophytes to sobriety didn't have the answers yet, they were still babes in the woods, but they were as clever and quick thinking as anyone I'd ever met. They had just been using their intelligence, or it was being used by the addiction, to manipulate themselves and others to continue their addictive behavior patterns.

Another fairy tale, one written by Hans Christian Anderson, "The Red Shoes," is viewed by many—including Clarissa Pinkola Estés in *Women Who Run with the Wolves* and by Kent and Maria Carr in their book *Unraveling Collective Confusion: Archetypes and Issues*[42]—as a tale about addiction.

The story is about a poor, motherless child who has no shoes. The child pieces together a pair of crude red shoes from scraps of cloth; she loves these shoes dearly. Subsequently, she gets adopted by a wealthy old woman, who throws her old crude red shoes out into the fire. The little girl gets very sad and upset about this. She learns the strict rules and manners of the society of the wealthy old woman, but in her heart she burns with desire for the lost red shoes she loved so much. For her religious confirmation in church, she selects a pair of the finest, most glowing red leather shoes you can imagine, even though they weren't really appropriate for the solemn religious ceremony. In fact, they were an outright scandal to all who saw them; even the icons on the walls of the church frowned (I can just picture this in a Disney movie), but the little girl did not care. All she could think about was her beautiful red shoes and how much she loved them.

The wealthy old woman is mortified and tells the little girl to never wear the red shoes to church again, but the little girl defies her and wears them to church the very next Sunday. At the entrance to the church an old, wounded soldier taps the soles of her shoes and tells her to "Remember to stay for the dance." Immediately an itch in her feet begins, and after church she starts to dance and cannot stop. She dances everywhere; she can't control her feet or stop the dancing. The old woman and her coachman finally pry the shoes off by force and the little girl's feet calm down. The old woman then takes the shoes and hides them away, while warning the little girl to never touch them again. And of course, the little girl cannot resist; she finds the hidden shoes, puts them on again, and the dancing begins again, and again it is out of her control. The shoes are dancing her and take her wherever they—not she—want to go. The little girl finally becomes terrified and tries to take the red shoes off, but she cannot even budge them.

She continues dancing on and on until she is completely exhausted and worn-out, but she still cannot stop the dancing. She becomes skin and bones; the red shoes are killing her. In desperation, she goes to the town executioner and asks him to chop off her feet—there is no other choice, no other way. He agrees and cuts off the feet of the little girl, with the red shoes on them. The shoes continue dancing and dance away with the little girl's amputated feet inside. She is now crippled for the rest of her life, serves others, and never again wishes for the red shoes! What a story!

The original red shoes the little girl loved so dearly, that she had pieced together from scraps of cloth, represent her authentic, instinctive creative attempt to nurture herself, to have some specialness in the absence of a real mother who loved her, who would have been able to mirror and mediate what she needed. The wealthy old woman did not appreciate the little girl's instinctive desire for specialness, and was a poor persona substitute for a real mother. She was much more concerned about what society would think than about what the little girl really needed.

We could say that the little girl's narcissistic desire for specialness grabbed onto something from the collective, the glowing red leather shoes, as a poor substitute for what she really needed and wanted. This is like so many alcoholics and addicted people who turn to the potentially addictive behavior, a poor substitute, to try to get what is missing in their lives (self-esteem, love, happiness, contentment, accomplishments, success, value, appreciation, etc.). Often the developmental background for addiction is full of missing pieces that a person is desperately trying to find or replace. When these pieces cannot be found in the real world, with real people and in real relationships with self and others, many look to fantasy replacements informed by society and the persona of the collective offered by celebrities, movies, magazines, and the media. Excessive consumption, materialism, and potentially addictive behaviors—using alcohol, drugs, food, sex, gambling, etc. to supply the missing pieces, to fill the void, even if only temporarily—are the route that many people take.

The second pair of red shoes are the addiction, which at first comforts and allows for diversion and escape, but then it becomes an all-consuming desire and obsession, so that nothing else matters. Clarissa Pinkola Estés says, "The girl begins to whirl and twirl her life away in a manner that, as with addiction, does not bring bounty, hope or happiness, but trauma, fear and exhaustion. There is no rest for her."[43]

As in an addiction, there is a point where she has lost control of the situation, is powerless, and her life has become unmanageable. The addiction, represented by the red shoes, is then completely in control, calling all the shots, and she is merely a puppet, doing what it dictates. This is where the ego-complex system is hijacked and completely taken over by the Addiction-Shadow-Complex. If this continues, only death and destruction and the loss of everything will follow.

Unless something extraordinary occurs to neutralize the addiction, then all is lost. In the story, this is represented as the drastic, mutilating, almost unthinkable act of cutting off the little girl's feet, her conscious standpoint, so that another standpoint, more humble and of service to others, can replace it. When this happens, the little girl becomes fully conscious of the diabolical nature of her addiction to the red shoes and, at least in the story, never wishes for them again.

The little girl saves her life by accepting what seems to the ego to be the worst possible fate, the sacrifice of the addicted ego point of view in its entirety. In A.A. this is all about Steps One, Two, and Three.

1. We admitted we were powerless over alcohol—that our lives had become unmanageable.
2. Came to believe that a Power greater than ourselves could restore us to sanity.
3. Made a decision to turn our will and our lives over to the care of God as we understood Him.

Sometimes the Power greater than ourselves is the executioner that cuts things off in a seemingly quick and brutal way (Stop drinking now!). Sometimes we have to turn over control and trust to the executioner (God, the A.A. community, the Twelve Steps, one's sponsor) without knowing for sure whether they will help save our lives or kill us. This is the kind of severe, extreme psychological surgery that we would all shy away from unless we had hit bottom, unless our lives had become so miserable and meaningless and intolerable and desperate that we could not go on any longer in this awful suffering and pain. The choices at this point are either suicide, where the addiction has its final victory over our existence, or else drastic, radical psychic surgery that might save our lives from the monster addiction. Tough choices!

Clarissa Pinkola Estés sees the second pair of red shoes as the potentially addictive behavior that indicates a loss of connection to authentic instinct. The little girl begins the fairy tale without a mother to protect and nurture, inspire and guide her. This void is ultimately filled by the excesses of the death-dealing vehicles of the addictive behavior, which eventually breaks all the psychic bones and ends in the total destruction and annihilation of the individual. The red shoes in the story also image the Archetypal Shadow/Archetypal Evil aspect of the Addiction-Shadow-Complex, which we cannot assimilate but can only distance ourselves from. Remember that the red shoes live on even without the little girl. Perhaps they will dance on until they find someone else to foolishly step in and wear them to his or her peril.

You may be wondering why I haven't referred to Dionysus from Greek mythology (Bacchus in Roman myth) in my discussion of alcoholism and addiction reflected in myth and fairy tales. I am not convinced that the story of Dionysus is relevant or even about alcoholism and addiction. It may be about excess and ecstasy and even about abuse, but not addiction. It is a very complicated myth with far-ranging implications and meanings. Some might argue that the Maenads (Bacchae), the wild women followers of Dionysus, represent the destructive dismemberment aspects of alcoholism and addiction, but these women were not, according to the myth, perpetually drunk and out of control. In fact, their behavior appeared to be contained and prescribed within the bounds of the collective religious ritual in which they were taking part.

Many people become aggressive and even violent when abusing alcohol. The primitive sexual and aggressive areas of the physiological old brain in humans, when stimulated with enough alcohol, activate, and are scientifically well documented, as well as the impairment to perception, concentration, and judgment when alcohol affects our brains. Perhaps the Maenads, in some of their aspects, are mythical representations of the human biological and psychological phenomena that occur when the peaceful, fun-loving, celebratory effects transform, with too much consumption, into the uninhibited, violent, murderous, and brutally aggressive sexual behavior that at times happens with drunkenness. When peaceful, the Maenads could touch rocks and earth and magically call forth springs of water, milk, and wine; suckle wild animals and babies; and bring forth streams of sweet honey from their *thyrsi* (pinecone-tipped staffs of Dionysus followers), but when they got into their intoxicated rage and madness, they could with tremendous physical strength turn in bloodthirsty abandon to tearing apart animals, trees, the earth, humans, and that same innocent life they had previously nurtured. Most violent crimes—assaults, murders, spouse and child abuse, and rape—are alcohol- and/or drug-related events. Most barrooms and apartments get torn up only when people have had too much to drink. Most fights at wedding receptions occur when people have gone well over their limit with alcohol. This is not coincidence. But as sad, destructive, and regrettable as these events are, they are about behaviors connected to excess and abuse, not necessarily to addiction.

The fact that people get looser—less inhibited socially, sexually, and aggressively—with alcohol consumption doesn't make them alcoholic or addicted, according to my definition. It may make them drunk and stupid and very embarrassed the next morning, but that doesn't mean they are incapable of ego control, moderation, or restraint in their use of alcohol, and it doesn't necessarily mean that Archetypal Shadow/Archetypal Evil is part of the picture. Perhaps the Maenads and other followers of Dionysus are there to make us conscious of how thin that line can be between ecstasy and drunken insanity when using alcohol.

There are also an abundance of creative and life-giving qualities attributed to Dionysus, not just his love of partying, but his involvement in teaching people farming techniques, as well as how to cultivate and make wine; he is also the god who inspired the birth of drama and theater in the Western world. He and Bacchus, his counterpart in Roman myth, may be the gods of drunkenness and merrymaking fools, but that still puts them a long way from Bluebeard, Iago, Satan, and the vampire in imaging Archetypal Shadow/Archetypal Evil. In any case, I have not found what I consider to be significant reflections of Archetypal Shadow/Archetypal Evil being played out in the myth of Dionysus.

Perhaps the most widely known myth image of Archetypal Evil today is from the hugely popular *Star Wars* movie, with the story of Anakin Skywalker, a jedi knight, wanting to do good, but being tempted by the seductions, deceptions, and inflations of the Dark Side of the Force until he succumbs and is rebirthed and renamed Darth Vader in his religious conversion and realignment with the transpersonal, archetypal powers of evil on the Dark Side.

Anakin, like many addicted people, tells himself and others that he can handle the energies and powers of the Dark Side, that he is in control and, for a while, he plays on the edge of the black hole, but he is in over his head from the beginning, and in the end he is no match for the Dark Side. He pays the price by having everything of value that he loves, including his wife, destroyed. The Dark Side uses his personal weaknesses—power, ambition, anger, and idealization—to entice him over, until it is too late and he is caught in the inescapable web of the Dark Side, which he now serves, under its complete control. This is wonderfully portrayed in the movie by the fact that Darth Vader is so mutilated as a human that he is literally reconstructed and resurrected by the Dark Side, with the majority of his body operated by machines. He is literally kept alive by the Dark Side; this includes the very air he breathes. Of course this is not done for his personal well-being, but so that his considerable powers and abilities can continue to be in service to the Dark Side.

Like those under the Addiction-Shadow-Complex, Darth Vader believes he has personal autonomy, willpower, and the ability to make individual choices and decisions, all of which were in reality lost long ago, but which the Dark Side, like the addiction, is capable of persuading and deluding the person into believing that he or she is still in control.

The Dark Side in *Star Wars* has all the qualities of a central, core kingdom of evil pitted against the Force, a core kingdom of good and light and hope, and once again human beings—and, in *Star Wars*, many other species—are caught between the transpersonal warring energies of the Force and the Dark Side.

Star Wars is very much a modern myth, reconfiguring the same archetypal elements of Lucifer and the fallen angels pitted against God, the Archangel Michael, and his army of angels (jedi knights), with all the humans in the middle, who can be recruited on either side. In the *Star Wars* myth the role of the Messiah, or Christ, is played by Luke Skywalker, with some very different Hollywood twists and turns, including the fact that Luke Skywalker's father turns out to be Darth Vader. As interesting as all this is, what is most important for our purposes is that *Star Wars* is another myth, modern though it be, that reflects and portrays images of Archetypal Shadow/Archetypal Evil in its dynamics.

The Lord of the Rings, by J. R. R. Tolkien, is the incredible epic fantasy adventure of the struggle of hobbits, dwarves, fairies, elves, trees, ents, trolls, humans and others to find their place in the universe, wrestling with the forces of prejudice, caste systems, war, species competition, survival, what is ultimately good or bad and, perhaps most importantly, what is the nature of evil on both the personal and the transpersonal level. In this story Archetypal Shadow/Archetypal Evil is imaged in its absolute form as Sauron, the most powerful evil being, a spirit who brings total death, total darkness, total destruction wherever he rules. His dominating power is so awesome it obliterates the very existence of all light and life. When Sauron rules, all is darkness and death (another image of the black hole).

Against such an all-powerful spirit-being, the hobbits—Bilbo Baggins, Frodo Baggins, Sam Gamgee, and a host of others—battle, many times reluctantly, against overwhelming odds to save the earth, humanity, nature, and life itself. Often the task seems hopeless, especially with relatively small, peace-loving hobbits being assigned much of the redeeming and saving of it all. Very much as in a true addiction, the odds often seem hopeless against the overwhelming darkness, death, and destruction manifest in the Archetypal Shadow/Archetypal Evil aspect of the Addiction-Shadow-Complex.

Frodo, the primary hero in the story, is wounded by evil and suffers continually with the wound and the burden of the accursed Ring of Power that he must return to its source to be destroyed in the fires of Mount Doom. He is tempted, tortured, close to despair, and is almost killed many times along the way. His protection and salvation is through gifts and powers bestowed on him by friends and higher sources of goodness and grace (his Higher Power).

Most alcoholics and addicted individuals did not consciously choose to be in the arena with Archetypal Shadow/Archetypal Evil, and like the hobbits find themselves reluctantly in an overwhelming, seemingly hopeless battle to save themselves, their marriages, their families, their businesses, and their communities. Similarly, as in the *Lord of the Rings* story, the way through involves humility (the humble hobbits) as the correct psychological attitude to take, and being guided one step at a time (as the hobbits were) by the transpersonal higher forces and powers of light and goodness and healing against the higher forces and powers of darkness, evil, and death. The battle against Sauron and his legions is, for the alcoholic or addicted individual, the same as the battle against Archetypal Shadow/Archetypal Evil in the addiction.

One of the beliefs in A.A., based on practical, firsthand experience about alcoholism, is that once you are alcoholic (addicted) then you will always be so. They say alcoholics are always just one drink away from reactivating the addiction, no matter how long they have been sober. A person's choice is between being an active, using alcoholic or being a sober, recovering alcoholic. There is no third option of being a former alcoholic. I believe that what this is all about is that, once a person has been touched by the ultimate Archetypal Shadow/Archetypal Evil in alcoholism, there is left a permanent indelible mark and vulnerability that is carried from then on for the rest of one's life. Once you have crossed that line, there is no going back. There is always the latent potential for reactivation of the addiction.

It is something like the reverse of the belief that a positive indelible character or mark is conferred at Christian baptism, which claims, initiates, and activates a person as a Christian from that point on for the rest of one's life, regardless of whether the person practices the Christian faith or not. Christian confirmation, as a sacrament, is also believed to activate the Holy Spirit in a special way that is a permanent potential for spiritual growth, regardless of whether the person uses it or not. So is the awakening of the Kundalini in the Hindu tradition, which is believed to permanently awaken and activate the spiritual, psychological, and physical energies of potential transformation in the individual. If the highest spiritual forces of goodness and grace can leave these kinds of permanent effects, it seems logical to suppose that the most powerful forces of destruction and evil can in some way do likewise in the opposite direction.

I don't believe this idea of once an alcoholic always an alcoholic, once addicted always addicted, is about some kind of deep-rooted paranoia, defeatism, battered self-esteem, or a perpetual victimization mentality. I believe it reflects the fact that once a person has been touched by the Archetypal Shadow/Archetypal Evil aspect of addiction, this exposure and proximity to such powerful, lethal, and unitegratable dark destructive energy leaves a perpetual marker, scar, and vulnerability, like being exposed to super-powerful, deadly psychological nuclear radiation, which leaves an eternal residue in the cells of the body and of the psyche. Any further exposure to the radiation could reactivate the lethal toxicities and result again in sickness and even death. Once exposed, there is always the potential danger of reactivation with any further exposure.

The *Harry Potter* series, written by J. K. Rowling and translated wonderfully in film, is another popular modern myth reflecting aspects of Archetypal Shadow/Archetypal Evil in the story line about the young English boy magician or wizard, Harry Potter, and his lengthy and perilous educational adventures in using and discerning the magic powers of good and evil, healing and destruction, in diverse worldly and otherworldly realms. In the story, Harry's parents, good wizards, are killed by Lord Voldemort, the most powerful, evil archwizard who rules over a host of evil minions who carry out his ambitious plans to destroy all good and become the all-powerful dictator over everything. One group of these subordinates is known as the Dementors, creatures who search out, suck dry, extract and destroy the very soul essences of other beings, under the direction of Lord Voldemort.

It is only the love of Harry's mother that protects him and allows Harry to survive Lord Voldemort's attacks, which were intended to kill him. He escapes death, but is left with a perpetual scar/wound from this experience, his indelible mark, which continues to resonate with pain and suffering anytime he comes near or in contact with any evil associated with Lord Voldemort (the stories' version of Archetypal Shadow/Archetypal Evil). As with the Fisher King in the Grail legend, the scar is an eternal wound that seems never to heal. Or the affliction of St. Paul, whatever it is, that the Lord refuses to take away and so Paul must learn to live with the affliction and its continuous torment.

Harry, like the recovering alcoholic, has been touched by Archetypal Shadow/Archetypal Evil and it has left a permanent scar and vulnerability, which must be suffered, but also allows Harry and recovering alcoholics and addicted individuals to know this kind of evil on a personal, intimate, first-name basis. This wisdom and knowledge may be what saves humanity, in the final analysis, from Lord Voldemort and the Dementors of this world.

This knowledge is like the price many exorcists in the Catholic Church report that they must pay for wrestling with the transpersonal evil energies of the Devil, which remain somehow always with them, physically and psychologically. Perhaps this is why the best sponsors in A.A. are those who have been to hell and back. They are the epitome of the effectiveness and the necessity of the wounded healer. The power of addiction to destroy lives should never be minimized or underestimated.

Probably the best image of Archetypal Shadow/Archetypal Evil in myth, fairy tales, and religion is that of the Devil. Even Jung, in his letter to Bill W., chooses to describe this almost irresistible "power of evil" in addiction as the Devil. I don't believe Jung used this image casually or without great awareness of what he was pointing towards. I believe he was very conscious and intentional in using the Devil to describe an essential, crucial aspect of the phenomenon of alcoholism and addiction.

In many fairy tales, the Devil can be redeemed. In one Grimm's tale to which von Franz refers, "The Prince and the Princess," it is the Devil's daughter who has a human heart and saves the helpless man from the irresistible evil of her father, the Devil. These kinds of tales image where Eros and consciousness and connection with the Self can help the individual to integrate, overcome, and transform destructive personal shadow aspects of the psyche. Perhaps these tales refer to mental/emotional disorders that can be overcome and healed. Perhaps they signal the hope that we are still able to stop and change alcohol and drug behavior at the abuse stage, potentially preventing addiction where we have not yet crossed that line.

There are other tales of the Devil where there is no possibility of overcoming the darkness, the core evil, the Archetypal Shadow/Archetypal Evil represented by this form of the Devil. In one myth, a version of the story of the origin of the Devil, all the devils were initially angels of the Lord in heaven, worshipping, praising, and adoring him, and doing God's will above and below. God had created the angels with free will, so they were able to choose freely whom they would serve and what allegiance they would have.

One day, as the story goes, God decided to create human beings out of the mud of creation and also to give humans free will to listen to God or not. Humans were being offered a potential place next to God in heaven, almost on a par with the angels. This so infuriated and insulted some of the angels, especially Lucifer, their leader, whose name means "bringer of light," that they decided to revolt and rebel against God's plan. They couldn't believe that God would give free will and the chance to be one with him in eternity to such lowly, crude, ugly, and muddy creatures. Because the angels were pure spirits, who would live forever, their choices and decisions, unlike those of humans, were also eternal. They could see the whole picture at once, so there was no changing of their minds. It's not as though at some point, like humans, they would realize something new or see that they had made a mistake. It also upset them—in their pride which cometh before a fall—that these finite, lowly humans would potentially be redeemed and elevated by God to an exalted eternal status, which previously only the angels were privileged to occupy. God had just gone too far this time, and they resented the hell out of it.

So they made their eternal choice to separate themselves from God and his divine plan. They have no regrets. Because of this eternal decision, these angels were kicked out of heaven; Michael, the good archangel, made sure it was so. Not being allowed to continue to reside in heaven, Lucifer created his separate domain in hell with other fallen angels, now called devils. There they perpetually plot, sabotage, and try to thwart God's plans by roaming the earth and tempting, manipulating, influencing, deceiving, and ultimately taking the souls of human beings away from God to damnation in their kingdom.

Whether or not you buy this story as some kind of an imaging of what really has happened, what is most significant about the image, energy, and spirit of Lucifer and the devils in this story is that they are, by their own choice, not transformable, redeemable, integratable, or savable anymore by God, goodness, or human intentions. The inherent hostility and malevolence at their core is now committed to the destruction and downfall of human beings by any means possible. They play by no rules but their own. Humans, without the aid of spiritual powers from God and the good angels, don't stand a chance against eternal spirits of such evil intention and power.

What is it that happens to decent, ethical, morally good human beings that transforms them, under the power of addiction, to abandon all the values and principles they have lived by and believed in? What force is so strong, so pervasive, so complete in possessing these formerly good human beings that it mutates them regardless of their personal backgrounds, beliefs, and histories into liars, cheaters, and thieves; into deceptive, dishonest, untrustworthy, despicable human beings? What kind of a malignant spirit then continues and perpetuates this destructive course of action until the human being, his health, his marriage, his family, his career, his friendships, and his very life are destroyed? Call this phenomenon what you will, but I agree with

Jung that the Devil fits the bill quite well—as a murderer from the beginning, as the great deceiver, as the father of all lies.

Linda Leonard describes addiction as the bondage of one's soul to the Devil. She envisions the devil in addiction as "The Moneylender," who we keep borrowing from, going deeper and deeper into hopeless debt, until he owns us completely and then he demands that we pay up. Here's how she describes the devil in addiction: "First of all he is in our psyche—that figure in us who convinces us we can have something for nothing, a free ride to paradise, a shortcut to creativity. For an addict, he is behind every glass of wine, every line of cocaine, every cigarette, every mounting debt, every romance that keeps us spellbound and remains untransformed into love, every power play. In the beginning the Moneylender [Devil] may seem friendly, even kindly. But once we are in debt his cruelty and demonic power often astound us. In the end we pay far more than we receive. And sometimes we pay with our lives."[44]

Jeffrey Burton Russell, a professor of history and religion presenting at Harry Wilmer's symposium on "Facing Evil," says of the Devil: "If the Devil does exist, what is he? If the concept has any meaning at all, he is the traditional Evil One—a mighty person with intelligence and will whose energies are bent on the destruction of the cosmos and the miseries of its creatures."[45]

Von Franz, echoing these thoughts, says that the Devil in some tales "is an intrinsically evil nature spirit who derives pleasure from destruction and murder for their own sake. It is dreadful to think that there is something of the sort in the unconscious human psyche, but the testimony of myths and fairy tales shows this to be the simple fact."[46]

Sometimes when I have made presentations on this dark, depressing, terrifying, and seemingly hopeless material about Archetypal Shadow/Archetypal Evil, people ask me, almost in despair, "What then can we do?" I will go further into answering this question in the next chapter on "The Healing Process of Recovery through the Twelve Steps of A.A.," but for now, while we are still in the fairy tale, mythical realm, let me share with you what von Franz offers us from her storehouse of knowledge and experience on the subject. She says, "Anyone who can enter into the innermost center of his own psyche, his Self, is safe against the assaults of the dark powers."[47] I am not so sure about this, unless by this "innermost center" she means entering into the Holy of Holies, into sacred space so to speak, where transpersonal spiritual powers are accessed and activated to neutralize the "assaults of the dark powers." Von Franz goes on to say that "Divine wholeness is the strategic 'weak point' of the evil one. That is where he has his heart or his 'death,' that is where he can be destroyed."[48] She relates how in many fairy tales the Devil or Evil One keeps his heart hidden on an island, in a church or well, or in a duck or an egg: all of these are symbols of wholeness and of the true Self.

Two important ideas are suggested by von Franz's comments here. One, that the effects of Archetypal Shadow/Archetypal Evil can only be canceled out or neutralized by spiritual wholeness or archetypal good and light—which would mean the archetype of the Self in Jungian terms or the Higher Power in A.A. Two, that in the final analysis Archetypal Shadow/Archetypal Evil, though intentionally hidden in the wholeness of the Self to deceive and disguise, is somehow still contained in and superseded by the Self. This idea has been echoed in many myths where both good and evil emanate from a unified supreme god figure, who allows the cosmic clash to unfold with the knowledge that in the end good will prevail, but often after much struggle and turmoil and hardship is visited upon human beings caught in the middle.

So there is encouragement that we are not completely at the mercy of the forces of Archetypal Shadow/Archetypal Evil, but we must not try to fight or deal with it as individuals through the puny power of our inflated egos, but through an alignment with the greatest spiritual powers of love and goodness and light we can find.

It is interesting to note how often the Eros principal of love and deep human relationships as protective, healing, and neutralizing of evil has come up so far in this book. In Jung's letter to Bill W., Eros is "the protective wall of human community" that Jung says "can counteract the evil principle [Archetypal Shadow/Archetypal Evil] prevailing in this world." The young man mentioned earlier, who had the great final showdown dream with God and the Devil battling it out in the domed cathedral in St. Louis, was saved and led out of danger by the kind, good, yet imperfect divorced woman (Eros). Guggenbühl-Craig argues that what is missing in the psychic makeup of the psychopath is a chronic, unhealable deficiency and lack of Eros.

In the Red Shoes fairy tale imaging addiction, what is missing from the very beginning for the little girl is the special nurturing Eros love of her mother. In the Harry Potter story it is only Harry's mother's love (Eros) which saves him from being killed by Lord Voldemort as a young child. Von Franz points to the need in fairy tales to find the hidden heart of the Devil, or evil, to destroy it (if that is possible). The heart has always represented the Eros principal. Finally, the Eros principle is manifested in A.A. through the fellowship of other recovering alcoholics in their loving, caring support and assistance for each other. Part of the antidote to Archetypal Shadow/Archetypal Evil certainly seems to be an activated Eros principle within the human community.

The assertion of the existence of Archetypal Shadow/Archetypal Evil raises many theoretical philosophical, theological, and psychological questions. Saying that Archetypal Shadow/Archetypal Evil is ultimately an aspect of the wholeness of the Self, for example, explains and clarifies no more than saying God created all things and therefore created evil, and evil is then, somehow, an aspect or part of God. Some would describe evil as the shadow or dark side of God. This may all be true in the final analysis and in the heavenly realms, but it does not help humans to understand or deal any better with the Devil (if there is one) or Archetypal Shadow/Archetypal Evil in this world. These kinds of theoretical macrocosmic explanations appear to me to be beyond our finite human intellectual comprehension. Even if it is ultimately part of the divine plan, it is still so deadly and toxic to humans we cannot touch it, integrate, metabolize, or process it as humans. Even worse, if it can kill and completely destroy us, divine plan or not changes nothing. So whether we place Archetypal Shadow/Archetypal Evil within or without the psyche, or partially within and partially without, it is truly experienced as transpersonal to us and needs to be guarded against, avoided at all costs and, when encountered, neutralized.

I don't want to get into the presently unresolvable theoretical debate among Jungians and others about whether everything, including the archetypes, is completely contained within the Self/psychic system of humans, or whether there are things, including the archetypes, that derive from another external source—an objective "other" somehow outside of or beyond us but which is somehow imaged in us, and part of us, manifesting in one way as the archetypes.

This theoretical psychological debate very much mirrors the same presently unresolvable theological debate about the nature and existence of God. People come down arguing on all sides—theists who affirm God's existence and atheists who deny God's existence and agnostics who don't know one way or the other. Among the theists there are those who believe God and humans are a completely unified oneness; there are those who believe God to be completely separate, independent, superior and external to humans, but that we may be able to relate to, communicate with, and petition him/her/it; and then there are those who believe that God is much bigger, greater, and more comprehensive than humans, but that humans are imbued with some of the divine aspects of God. In Judeo-Christian tradition, this would be the idea that we humans are all created somehow in the image and likeness of God referred to in Genesis. There are others who believe a combination of these theories. Still others believe there is a God, but it is a great, unknowable mystery full of paradox and Zen-like koans.

Once again, as fascinating as this speculative theology and the question about the origins and creation of the archetypes is, it digresses from our primary phenomenological concern with the nature of true addiction, specifically the existence of Archetypal Shadow/Archetypal Evil as a key ingredient necessary for an addiction to exist. I cannot answer the origin of the archetypes question, in fact I have nothing new to contribute regarding it, but I can assert from observation and experience with addictions that there is a transpersonal (beyond the individual), deadly archetypal phenomenon that is not educable, healable, or integratable by humans, which I have chosen to label Archetypal Shadow/Archetypal Evil. I make no further assertions or speculations about where it came from, whether it exists in other realms and dimensions, and where it is ultimately heading. These are just not germane to the central question of addiction as a psychic phenomenon. In fact, such fascinating questions and speculations can easily distract and take the focus away from trying to understand the psychodynamics of addiction.

Again, I can truly appreciate Jung's hesitancy to wade into the discussion about the diabolical archetypal dynamics of addiction until the very end of his life. It is almost as though what he did in his letter to Bill W. was that he stopped, just when he was about to leave this world, turned back at the last moment, and hesitatingly threw us this bomb and said, "Now you guys deal with it! I've done enough. I am outta here."

Phenomenologically acknowledging the existence of Archetypal Shadow/Archetypal Evil as an inintegratable, transpersonal phenomenon in the psychodynamics of addiction is all I'm asking you to consider, and it is plenty by itself.

WHY PEOPLE ARE DRAWN TO ARCHETYPAL SHADOW/ ARCHETYPAL EVIL

If Archetypal Shadow/Archetypal Evil is so frighteningly dangerous and destructive, it raises the question of why people would be drawn to it in the first place. From my experience and knowledge of Archetypal Shadow/Archetypal Evil in alcoholism and other addictions, I believe that people are drawn to it because of its allure of incredible power and energy, of unimaginable freedom, of the ultimate fulfillment of a desire for status, mastery, and prestige, and of the promise of superhuman potency.

The archetypes in general have always tempted humans with the fantasy and possibility that we might become gods. The vampire's allure is erotic and promises eternal life, though it be of the living dead. The Devil tempts Jesus in the Scriptures with power, possessions, and desires fulfilled, which the Devil seems able to provide. All Jesus needs to do is bow down before Satan. Many addicted people tell of histories and experiences of complete inadequacy and impotency without their fix. Some men and women have no social courage or confidence without alcohol or drugs, but with them they feel invincible and powerful and self-assured.

Bill W. told the story of his first drink to Robert Thomsen, his biographer. Thomsen relays the incredibly numinous, powerful, ecstatic, and panacean nature of Bill's experience:

> Perhaps it took a little time, but it seemed to happen instantly. He could feel his body relaxing, a stiffness going out of his shoulders as he sensed the warm glow seeping through him into all the distant, forgotten corners of his being. ... Soon he had the feeling that he wasn't the one being introduced but that people

were being introduced to him; he wasn't joining groups, groups
were forming around him. It was unbelievable. And at the sud-
den realization of how quickly the world could change, he had
to laugh and he couldn't stop laughing. ...
It was a miracle. There was no other word. A miracle that was
affecting him mentally, physically, and, as he would soon learn,
spiritually too.
Still smiling, he looked at people around him. They were not
superior beings. They were friends. They liked him and he liked
them. ...
[When he left,] at his back he could hear the whine of a saxo-
phone, little waves of voices rising, falling, but now they in no
way ran against the overwhelming joy he was feeling. His world
was all around him, young and fresh and loving, and as he made
his way down the drive he moved easily, gracefully, as though—
he knew exactly how he felt—all his life he had been living in
chains. Now he was free.[49]

Bill W. had, I believe, an archetypal experience with his first drink of
alcohol. It activated a thirst in him to forever recapture that freedom,
that perfect moment and feeling. The alcohol connected him with the
false self and opened the door ultimately to the Archetypal Shadow/
Archetypal Evil in his alcoholism. Bill was on a Grail quest, he was
thirsting for the true spirit, "the highest religious experience," as Jung
put it, but he got hopelessly caught up in the lies and false promises
of the depraving poison of the spirits of alcohol until he discovered
A.A., the Higher Power, and the true Self.

Some men and women literally cannot perform sexually without
their addiction to empower their penises, vaginas, and sexual allure.
One recovering alcoholic man I've worked with for a number of years
tells how tortuously shy, introverted, and completely inadequate and
worthless he had felt throughout his childhood into his adult life.
He says that alcohol saved his life for a time, in the sense that without it he never would have been able to function in the outer world.
He never would have been able to relate to others socially, in school
or at work. He never would have been able to find a mate and have
a family. Alcohol for him was the best, most powerful and influen-
tial friend he had for many years, until it demanded he sacrifice
everything, including his soul, on its altar. He had been thankful to

alcohol for supplying him with energy and drive and spirit when it was so sorely lacking in him. It was fine until the "cure" began killing him. The problem with selling your soul to the Devil, or addiction, is not the benefits you get in the short run, it is the ultimate price you must pay. The short-term payoff is often worth it; it's the long-term consequences that relativize the equation, because it is ultimately a deal with death.

Jung knew and continually cautioned against ego overidentification with the archetypes in general. He described the inflation, the seductiveness, the irresistibility of the archetype, and how we must try to stay grounded and humble and human against the overwhelming temptation to potentially become one of the gods or goddesses. If not, we could be mortally wounded, crippled, dismembered, struck with madness or ultimately destroyed.

Fairly recent, well-known societal examples of this dangerous overidentification with the archetypes can be found in Marilyn Monroe, the famous film star and pin-up girl who overidentified with and tried to carry the impossible projection of being Aphrodite, the Greek goddess of sex and love, for everyone male and female on the planet. No wonder it resulted in broken relationships, in disappointment and unbearable stress, as well as outrageous expectations of herself and from others. She abused alcohol and drugs to escape from the pressure, and in trying to cope with so much she was finally destroyed in 1962 at the age of thirty-six by a drug overdose of sleeping pills, probably in an attempt to get away from it all. She has since been elevated into the pantheon of cultural icons and resides now as the forever unchangeable sex goddess of our time. It only cost her her life as a human being.

Elvis Presley, another cultural icon in our modern pantheon, is also an example of the dangers of archetypal overidentification with the Gods. As a talented singer, performer, musician, and rock-and-roll-sex-symbol star, he was the "King," the Adonis of his time. And like Adonis from Greek mythology, who was young, handsome, and sexy, the masculine counterpart to the feminine sex goddess, Aphrodite, who loved him and found him irresistible, Elvis had the same irresistibility for most women. Everyone adored him and wanted, literally and figuratively, a piece of him. It ultimately killed him. He died in 1977 from a drug overdose. He massively abused legally prescribed stimulants and sedatives so that he could perform and function, and carry the burden of being "the king of rock and roll" with all the crazy, unrealistic projections and expectations of his fans and admirers weighing down on him. Elvis is another sad, tragic story of being destroyed by overidentification with the archetypes.

The English Princess Diana, called "Princess Di" in a fondly familiar way by her fans, admirers, and the media, crumbled under the archetypal projection to be the perfect, beautiful, happy-ever-after fairy tale princess for the whole world, which, of course, was impossible.

There is actually not a very good track record of survival for humans who overidentify with the archetypes. It is a very dangerous business. No wonder Jung was so adamant about the prohibition of this, to protect us. When we identify with an archetype, with the gods, our inflation, infatuation, and possession doesn't allow us to be normal, finite, and human, to function like other mere mortals. This is why all the great saints and mystics have so emphasized being grounded in humility—they were being constantly tempted to an inflated overidentification with the divine and to forgetting their humanness. True humility is the antidote to archetypal inflation for humans. This inflation certainly is a potential danger for alcoholics and addicted individuals, this narcissistic specialness that tells them that they are different, that they are the exception, that the rules do not apply to them. It is easy to begin to delusionally believe that we are a special category of human being, entitled to more, and different than others—to begin to think we are a god. If this happens, it is only a matter of time before the hubris calls forth the archetypal compensation from the gods to take us down and to put us in our proper place.

In myth and fairy tales humans are always punished severely or killed for stealing from, infringing upon, or trying to be a god or goddess. Some, like Prometheus, who brought fire to humans, and Aesculapius, who healed the sick and raised the dead, made contributions to humanity, but they personally paid for it very dearly. Prometheus was sentenced to being chained to a mountain while an eagle continually ate away his regenerating liver (what a metaphor) until Hercules finally freed him. Aesculapius was killed for his transgressions, and was eventually welcomed into the pantheon of Greek gods because of humanity's massive outcry to Zeus over his death. Most human overidentification with the archetypes is selfish, egocentric, and pedestrian; it does not contribute to the betterment of humanity in any way, but the price that must be paid is the same.

These are the potential consequences of ego overidentification with "any" archetype—just imagine the consequences of upping the ante to the ultimate archetype of Evil, of Archetypal Shadow, where nothing is integratable, nothing can be assimilated, nothing can be transformed on the human level—we have about as much chance as a snowball in hell.

CLARIFICATION OF DEFINITIONS OF ARCHETYPAL SHADOW/ ARCHETYPAL EVIL

The terms Archetypal Shadow or Archetypal Evil have been used by different people in different ways, sometimes meaning very different things. For example, Liliane Frey-Rohn uses the term Archetypal Evil to represent collective shadow in society and as a synonym for the shadow aspect or dark side of all the archetypes, including personal shadow, persona, anima, animus, hero, mother, etc. She views Archetypal Evil as coming out of the imbalance or one-sidedness of the social, collective, cultural situation, not as individual, but as impersonal and plural in nature.[50] Her use of the term Archetypal Evil has a different meaning from the way I use it. She does not address the unintegratable aspects of the phenomena as I see it.

I believe it is this psychologically unintegratable aspect of addiction, which I call Archetypal Shadow/Archetypal Evil, which distinguishes and makes alcoholism and addiction in some ways fundamentally different from most other forms of mental/emotional disorders. It is this unintegratable aspect that is essential and inherent to my use of the term, because it explains that aspect of addiction that is immune to any forms of ego insight, ego control, or ego adaptation.

Once again, as a phenomenologist, I am just trying to find the appropriate words and images to adequately describe the phenomenon. I'm trying to create a map that accurately reflects and names, as best I can, the true nature of addiction. I am not necessarily wed to the labeling. If better words can be found to describe this profoundly important aspect of addiction, I am open to using them.

There are terms in philosophy, theology, and literature such as "radical evil," "real evil," "absolute evil," "core evil," "objective evil," "transcendent evil," and "transpersonal evil" that all point to an aspect of evil, or a type of evil, that goes beyond personal sin and weakness and wrongdoing. They all allude to a source or realm of evil bigger, deeper, more powerful and profound than that generated by the individual human being. They all point in some way to the phenomenon I am talking about as Archetypal Shadow/Archetypal Evil, which is an essential component in the construction of the psychodynamics of psychological addiction.

There is something in the nature of the phenomenon of addiction that is clearly and substantially different from what is going on in many other kinds of mental/emotional psychiatric disorders, something that is not explained by existing theories and psychodynamic models of traditional egocentric psychologies—even definitions of neurosis and psychosis don't capture adequately what is going on in addiction. There is something darker and more sinister than our traditional views of mental illness.

As sad, tragic, and debilitating as schizophrenia and bipolar disorders can be, there is still a sense of hopeful humanness that underlies them, and they can be and are impacted in a positive way, sometimes significantly, by different forms of psychotherapy and psychopharmacology. In depression, obsessive compulsive disorders, bipolar disorder, schizophrenic disorders, personality disorders, and adjustment disorders there is no absolute initial treatment requirement, for its effectiveness, that there be an ego-collapse conversion experience—that a person admits complete powerlessness and that they turn to a higher-power authority in the psyche to heal them. In fact, in all these other mental/emotional disorders it is often necessary, helpful, and even required that the existing ego-complex system be strengthened, deepened, expanded, and more greatly empowered to do its job effectively. Traditional psychotherapy can be very effective in helping the patient to do this.

In many of these mental/emotional disorders (clinical depression, obsessive compulsion, bipolar, and schizophrenia) psychopharmacological medication is primary, necessary, and required for the effective treatment of the conditions, which is not true in treating addictions. Detox medication, Antabuse, and newer medications such as Naltrexone (ReVia) and Campral (which may turn out to be very helpful in suppressing or blocking the neurochemical effects of alcohol and others drugs in the brain by reducing or inhibiting their bio-logical craving effects), all can be helpful aids in treating alcoholism and addiction, but none of them is primary, necessary, and required, and none of them can arrest or cure an addiction on their own.

Some psychopharmacological medications can, on their own, cure if not arrest for long periods of time many of the worst, most debili-tating and prevalent forms of mental illness. Many mental/emotional disorders (reactive depression, obsessive compulsion, anxiety and ad-justment disorders) can be improved, arrested, or cured completely by traditional psychotherapies alone. Alcoholism and other addictions cannot initially be improved, arrested, or ever cured by traditional psychotherapy alone.

There is a manageability to most mental/emotional disorders other than addiction. Presently, almost all of them can be treated effectively with a combination of medications and psychotherapy. Medication and psychotherapy have not proven effective primary treatments in arresting alcoholism and addiction. They can be helpful aids at times in the recovery process, especially if there are other mental/emotional disorders involved (dual diagnosis) or in conjunction with the addic-tion that needs to be treated. Traditional psychotherapy and psycho-analysis can be helpful, especially once the addictive behavior has stopped and a recovering individual wants to work on developmen-tal, personality, and personal dynamics involved in contributing to and creating the addiction.

These differences in treatment approaches and effectiveness point phenomenologically to basic core differences in the nature of addic-tions (both psychologically and physiologically) and other mental/emotional disorders. In general, in neurosis the ego-complex system, though it is distorted and diminished in its functioning ability be-cause of chronic doubts, fears, and anxieties, continues to be able to function and do its job in the psyche. The ego is still capable of pro-cessing, adapting, integrating, and healing. In psychosis, the ego-com-plex system literally drowns in unconscious material, shuts down, sometimes completely, and is incapable of functioning effectively and doing its job. Of course, in both neurosis and psychosis there are vary-ing degrees of relative ego dysfunction involved for different individuals at different times. But in contrast to neurosis and psychosis, the ego-complex system in addiction continues to function, often on a very high level, but it is not the same ego-complex system of the person that was operating prior to the addiction taking over. It is something else, something different, that is operating, that ultimately has a Dr. Jekyll/Mr. Hyde, self-destructive, addiction-perpetuating dynamic and directive.

With addictions, especially alcohol and drug addiction, we know that there is something that is immune to, and defies, human interventions of every kind—something so deep and dark and "evil feeling" that it resonates with a coldness, a distance, a despair, a hopelessness beyond human scientific understanding, something that we fear and something that we cannot comprehend.

This unreachability and untouchability in addiction is clearest in the sad and disappointed eyes of husbands and wives, daughters and sons, families and friends, as they watch in desperate, absolute futility their loved ones drifting hopelessly, sometimes slowly, but inevitably, into a walking death until the addiction finally takes them out of their misery and everyone else's too.

You can see it too in the eyes of men and women who are drowning in addiction, as their focus fades further and further away into some distant unseen place that they distractedly always seem so antsy to get to, but never do. Each step away, their connection with you, the world, and reality diminishes, until they are but mere shells of their former selves, walking zombies or emerging vampires who eventually can see no one and nothing except their next fix.

Compassion fatigue comes quickly with addiction—much more quickly than with other forms of mental illness. It is hard to have sympathy for "the devil," and when you don't believe in "the devil," then you blame the person who is possessed for not getting it under control, changing, doing better, fixing it. Of course this is just the powerlessness of which A.A. speaks, which is central to both Satanic possession and to true addiction.

In support of this position that Archetypal Shadow/Archetypal Evil does exist and resides as a key component in addiction, I offer the following summary of ideas and terms, some mentioned previously, which I believe are describing the same or very similar phenomena.

Von Franz points to the Devil in fairy tales and myth as being at times "intrinsically evil," representing "dark powers" that are unassimilable. Carl Jung agrees with this view of the Devil-energy, especially in alcoholism and addiction dynamics. Jacoby, Kast, and Riedel name this phenomenon "Real Evil." Clarissa Pinkola Estés acknowledges a "type of manifest evil" that is irredeemable. Harry Wilmer refers to "absolute Evil, archetypal Evil," which is neither personal nor organizational. Jeffrey Burton Russell calls it "the Devil, the Evil One," and believes it most certainly exists as a real phenomenon. Carl Kerenyi refers to it as "an archetype of evil" imaged in both myth and religion. Maya Angelou describes it as "a torrential force," as "powers in some dimension which we cannot imagine" in eternal conflict.

I believe the phenomenon of Archetypal Shadow/Archetypal Evil is real, as do many others, regardless of what name it is given. This kind of evil by any other name (begging the rose's pardon) would still be the same.

CHAPTER FOUR

The Healing Process of Recovery through the Twelve Steps of A.A.

The healing process of recovery through the Twelve Steps of A.A. is essentially an addressing, and undoing, of the process of the psychodynamic development of the addiction described in Chapter Two, but in reverse order—addressing first what occurred last in forming the addiction, which would be the neutralizing of the Archetypal Shadow/Archetypal Evil aspect, and then moving on to the undoing of the rest of the Addiction-Shadow-Complex, including addressing the specific causes and payoffs of the addictive behavior, taking responsibility for the personal shadow and its actions, reconfiguring a more realistic and congruous persona, and undoing the ego's mistaken identification with the false self.

There are essentially six stages involved in the healing and recovery from a psychological addiction. They all revolve around the establishment of a conscious ego connection with the true Self (or Higher Power) and the neutralizing of the Archetypal Shadow/Archetypal Evil aspects of addiction. The six stages correlate with different groupings of the Twelve Steps of A.A. (Please refer to the chart on page 98 throughout this chapter.)

Stage 1 – The Ego Disidentifies with the Persona/False Self
Stage 2 – The Recognition of the Ego under Addiction-Shadow-Complex Control
Stage 3 – Relativizing of the Ego as the Center of the Psyche
Stage 4 – Confronting and Integrating the Personal Shadow

The Healing Process of Recovery through the Twelve Steps of A.A.

THE TWELVE STEPS

A

1. We admitted we were powerless over alcohol—that our lives had become unmanageable.

2. Came to believe that a Power greater than ourselves could restore us to sanity.

3. Made a decision to turn our will and our lives over to the care of God as we understood Him.

B

4. Made a searching and fearless moral inventory of ourselves.

5. Admitted to God, to ourselves, and to another human being the exact nature of our wrongs.

6. Were entirely ready to have God remove all these defects of character.

7. Humbly asked Him to remove our shortcomings.

8. Made a list of all persons we had harmed, and became willing to make amends to them all.

9. Made direct amends to such people wherever possible, except when to do so would injure them or others.

10. Continued to take personal inventory, and when we were wrong promptly admitted it.

C

11. Sought through prayer and meditation to improve our conscious contact with God as we understood Him, praying only for knowledge of His will for us and the power to carry that out.

12. Having had a spiritual awakening as the result of these steps, we tried to carry this message to alcoholics, and to practice these principles in all our affairs.

THE HEALING PROCESS AND RECOVERY – STAGES

A

1. Ego disidentifies with the persona/false self

2. Recognition of the ego under the Addiction-Shadow-Complex control

3. Relativizing of the ego as the center of the psyche

B

4. Confronting and integrating the personal shadow

C

5. Ongoing maintenance of the ego-Self axis

6. Living in service with the Self

Stage 5 – Ongoing Maintenance of the Ego-Self Axis
Stage 6 – Living in Service with the Self

A. TURNING IT OVER: THE FIRST THREE STEPS OF A.A. AND THE FIRST THREE STAGES OF THE PSYCHODYNAMICS OF RECOVERY

As bleak a picture as I've painted of addiction, which seems almost beyond hope and redemption, there is a way out, which A.A. found in the 1930s and which Carl Jung referred to in his letter to Bill W.: "*spiritus contra spiritum.*" The healing process, from a Jungian perspective, involves the development of a conscious ego connection with the authentic or true Self. Jungian psychology refers to it as the ego-Self axis. In A.A., it is the Higher Power to which alcoholics must surrender, and turn over their will and their lives to the care of God as they understand him. But first things first.

Step One of A.A. says: "We admitted we were powerless over alcohol—that our lives had become unmanageable." This first step is the key to all the other steps. Without this surrender or collapse or relativizing of the ego, the addicted individual is still stuck in the Addiction-Shadow-Complex where the addiction remains in control, calling the shots and dictating to the hijacked ego what it will think and feel and do. Remember that the prime directive of the addiction is to perpetuate itself at all costs, over every other agenda of life. As long as the addiction is still in control of the ego complex, the whole healing process remains depotentiated and in paralysis. Since the ego is infected, it is too weak, confused, and ineffective to truly fight or defeat the awesome power of the addiction.

The paradoxical solution is to surrender—to admit complete and utter defeat. At first, this seems like complete insanity. How could this possibly help—giving up, abandoning the field, and surrendering? The answer is in the psychodynamics of the situation. The addiction cannot function or continue to exert its power without the human ego to control as its host. It is much like the theology that asserts that without the freewill cooperation of human beings, God's power and effectiveness in the world is weakened, limited, or neutralized. In this sense, God is dependent and needs human beings to continue the work of his or her divine plan. Now, whether you agree with this theology or not, it is the model represented here that is of importance to us in understanding the addiction dynamic and its undoing.

The addicted individual, when he or she takes Step One of A.A., commits a version of ego-cide (a term created by David Rosen Jungian Analyst in his book and work on depression and suicide)—the person literally puts to death any attempt anymore to use this addicted ego to try to make judgments or choices or decisions or to take action related to addiction and recovery. The addiction is thus deprived of its "host organism," so to speak, in a parasitic sense.

Step One psychologically cuts off the food supply or the fuel for the addiction, and tries to save the person by starving the addiction and keeping the ego energy from being available to be used anymore by the addiction. The addiction grows, gets bigger and stronger, by getting the person to continue participating in the addictive behavior; if that stops, it creates a crisis for the addiction and its survival.

In this state of complete helplessness and collapse, which tempo-rarily puts the addiction out of business, the person still needs to live and breathe. Judgments, choices, decisions, and actions still need to be made and taken. Here is where the person must not only surren-der, but grab onto something else—or perhaps more aptly, completely accept and trust putting oneself in the hands and in the power and control of someone or something else. This leads us then to Step Two of A.A.

Step Two of A.A. reads: "Came to believe that a Power greater than ourselves could restore us to sanity."

This act of faith or belief completely undermines the manipula-tive deception of the Addiction-Shadow-Complex, which has worked long and hard to convince the addicted individual that it, the addic-tion, is God. Step Two challenges this false-idol assumption at its core; it is like driving the wooden stake into the heart of the vampire.

It is understandable that the addicted person would have come to view the addiction as divine. It is so numinous and powerful and overwhelming, and seemingly has all the answers. Psychologically, at the point in time where the person has crossed over from abuse to addiction, the ego has unknowingly surrendered everything to the addiction. The addiction becomes the ultimate authority and god in that person's psyche. It usurps the authority of the true Self and pro-claims itself to be divine and to be worshiped alone. It is of course a false god, built on an ego system that has already taken the wrong road by identifying with its persona, its false self. It is not that hard to go from a false self to a false god.

In Jungian terms, the Addiction-Shadow-Complex claims to be the true Self and the individual cannot tell the difference. The false god and the false self can only be unmasked and things put in their rightful place by the true Self, by the true Spirit of God (the true spirit of transpersonal goodness). The Archetypal Shadow/Archetypal Evil aspect of the addiction can *only* be neutralized by Archetypal Good and Archetypal Light from the highest spiritual sources of love and healing. There is no other way.

At this point in the recovery process, alcoholic or addicted individuals must blindly follow the principles and precepts of A.A.: go to meetings, listen to sponsors, stay away from temptation, and follow the guidance and advice of sober strangers who have trod this path before. They need to keep turning everything over to God, to keep reaffirming their powerlessness over the addiction, and not try to take it back and put it again under the control of their old addicted ego system—because if they do, the addiction will find an opening, a crack, a foothold by which to reenter and retake complete control of the person once again, the all-too-familiar relapse into the addictive behavior and reactivation of the Addition-Shadow-Complex.

Step Three in A.A., "Made a decision to turn our will and our lives over to the care of God as we understood Him," is crucial to neutralizing the Archetypal Shadow/Archetypal Evil aspect of the addiction, because only the most powerful, transpersonal, archetypal spiritual forces can counter and hold the massive diabolical forces of the addiction in check.

Step One is a negating, emptying-out step where we wholly give up, usually under duress, the illusion of our own power and control over the addiction and our lives. Step Two posits a theory of hope that there is something greater than us that can save us. It is a needed transitional step from the emptying, vacuumed position of Step One, but it is still on a speculative, belief-level basis. A decision of what to do has still not yet been made. Step Three is where the rubber meets the road. Step Three is where the recovering individual takes a positive-action step, a freewill decision not just to surrender and hope for hope, but to take personal responsibility for a positive plan of action. Many alcoholics and addicted individuals are full of un-acted-upon wishes, hopes, dreams, promises, and good intentions. Step Three challenges that "good intentions road to hell" very directly.

As one recovering alcoholic told me, Step One says "I can't," Step Two says "He Can," and Step Three says "I will let Him." Another analogy for Steps One, Two, and Three is that it is like watching a man on a tightrope pushing a wheelbarrow. At first we say, "He can't do it, he's gonna fall off" (Step One). Then we all see that he is doing it and can do it (Step Two)—observing the success other alcoholics are having following the program. But then the tightrope walker says, "OK, if you really believe I can do it, then climb into the wheelbarrow" (Step Three). There is no hedging your bet in Step Three, no holding on to remnants of ego and self-will. When we turn our will over to God or the Higher Power, we are freely giving up our right to call our own shots, to make our choices and decisions and actions based on what *we* think is right or the way *we* think it should be. Instead, we choose to continually defer our will and our lives, not to what *we* want, but to what God or the Higher Power or the Self wants from us. Step Three requires commitment, vigilance, and sustaining action of dependence upon God to call the shots in our lives.

Steps One and Two, unless reinforced by Step Three, the substantive action to fill the void they have created with something positive, will relatively quickly and easily lead back to frustration, hopelessness, and despair, which is fuel for the fire for the addiction, which will reassert its will as soon as the person is vulnerable and weak enough once again. In a sense, putting on the armor of God within and without (Step Three) is what protects us from being overtaken again by the addiction. It also prevents us from potentially being manipulated by the addiction, working through the still weakened and infected ego system to get to us. Step Three essentially says, "Put your money (your energies and efforts) where your mouth is. Don't just talk the talk, but walk the walk."

One of the recommended actions in A.A., for what they call "working the steps," is that for Step Three the recovering alcoholic literally finds a friend to join with him or her in prayer, asking for God's help in taking this step. Using the Higher Power to get to the Higher Power—pretty clever and, I understand, pretty effective too.

Step Three raises the question of the distinction between "free will" and "willpower" in the recovery process. Step Three clearly implies and assumes that "free will" exists for the alcoholic individual to be able to make a decision to turn his or her will and life over to the care of God as he or she understands him, even at this early stage in the process when the influence of Archetypal Shadow/Archetypal Evil is still overwhelmingly dominating and potentially all-powerful and controlling.

Free will is our ability to choose between alternatives so that the choice and action are to an extent creatively determined by us consciously. Willpower, on the other hand, is the strength of our will, mind, or determination, our self-control. Will itself is what we use to express determination, insistence, persistence—our willfulness. A.A. holds that free will is always present for the individual, it is never extinguished, but that willpower, the power of the will, which energizes and empowers free will, is not always present or sufficient to do what we say we want to do. Most alcoholics or addicted individuals struggle with this, and tell themselves they will not drink or take a drug or gamble right up until the time that they do. Free will remains, but there is not enough energy or power to overcome the overdetermining, compulsive power of the addiction.

The Addiction-Shadow-Complex is much like the myth of Pandora's Box: once it is unfortunately opened, everything gets released, or in the case of the Addiction-Shadow-Complex, everything falls under the spell and power of the addiction. In Pandora's story the one thing remaining in the box, the one thing saved, the one thing left, is hope. In addiction the one thing left, the one thing remaining, the one thing saved for the individual, is free will. Even Archetypal Shadow/Archetypal Evil cannot—as hard as it tries—extinguish free will. Free will is the hope, the key that opens the door to the future, both of sobriety and recovery.

The first three steps of A.A. correlate with the first three stages of the psychodynamics of the healing process and recovery. (On the chart on page 98 it is designated by the grouping of steps and stages categories under the letter "A".) This is where the ego system must undo its mistakes from the past. It must begin to *dis*-identify with the persona/false self (Stage 1). It must recognize and become conscious of the fact that it has been under the control of the Addiction-Shadow-Complex (Stage 2) and that it cannot trust its own judgment and perception of reality. The ego must in self-reflection realize that it is not the highest authority in the psyche—that the Self is the Highest Power in the psyche and that the ego should always subordinate its position and power and will to be in service to the true Self (Stage 3). This is what is meant by relativizing of the ego in the psychic hierarchy. This is always experienced by the ego as a defeat, a collapse, a blow, a deflation, a depressing realization, but it leads to the humility that can help save one's life. In A.A. it is about hitting bottom—the recognition of the hopelessness, futility, and misery of continuing on the arrogant, delusional path that one has been on. Bill W., referring to this part of the process, says, "You must always remember that 'hitting bottom' is the essence of getting hold of A.A.—really."[1]

I want to emphasize again that without Step One, putting the addicted ego out of commission, Steps Two and Three, as well as all the other steps of A.A., are not possible, because as long as the ego is contaminated and controlled by the Addiction-Shadow-Complex, and especially the influences of Archetypal Shadow/Archetypal Evil, it will twist and distort and manipulate any thoughts, feelings, insights, decisions, judgments, or actions toward continuation of the addictive behavior.

This idea of "hitting bottom," and giving up completely on getting sober through the abilities of the ego is not an archaic, outmoded notion of A.A. Psychodynamically, it is the most crucial and necessary step in initiating and setting into motion the only chance of healing and recovery possible for the alcoholic or addicted individual—without it, everything else becomes futile and ineffective.

Dr. Bob, one of the cofounders of A.A., who led the development of the Akron Group (one of the first two A.A. groups, the other being in New York City with Bill W.), actually required of prospective A.A. members an initial act of surrender of their egos, in which they had to get down literally on their knees in a dramatic symbolic gesture and say a prayer acknowledging their powerlessness over alcohol and their reliance upon God (the Higher Power) before they could attend an A.A. meeting—talk about a ritual to humble the ego!

This practice did not continue, as A.A. did not want to put any obstacles in the way of people joining the program who had a desire to stop drinking, no matter if they were believers, nonbelievers, atheists, or agnostics. The ritual is no longer required, but the essential surrender of the ego still is.

Another illustration of this phenomenon is the fundamental psychological "conversion experience" that Dr. Tiebout wrote about extensively and that Carl Jung had recommended to Roland H. It is the same essential neutralizing of the ego that is under the power of the Addiction-Shadow-Complex.

Some people have wondered why, for the most part, normal church activities and "taking the pledge" didn't and doesn't work in getting and keeping sobriety among alcoholics and addicted individuals, for these approaches also employ God and the spiritual in their efforts. The answer, from a psychodynamic perspective, is that the well-intentioned church activities and the "taking of the pledge" to not drink or use presumes a normal, healthy-enough ego capable of effecting change through willpower, insight, self-discipline, and ego control. In the rare cases where church or "the pledge" have been successful, my guess is that one of two things has happened: one, that the behavior was abuse and not addiction to begin with, where the ego still does have some power and control to effect change, or, two, the addicted person in the process of the church activities or "taking the pledge" unknowingly collapses and surrenders the addicted ego so that he or she can be affected and influenced by the spiritual forces that can help and make a difference. But without the consciousness of what this is about, there is the danger and overwhelming probability of a short-lived sobriety, as the addiction wheels and deals and finds a way to reactivate the addicted ego to do its bidding. This is probably what happened in the case Jung referred to in the *Collected Works* as "the man cured by Jesus," who initially got sober, but soon relapsed.

A clinical social worker colleague of mine teaches a smoking cessation class to the public through a local hospital. The approach of the class is a combination of education and behavior modification to help people stop smoking and remain abstinent. He has found that while the class is in progress it does help some people initially to stop smoking, but only for a brief time. It is not effective in most cases for helping people to maintain their abstinence in the long run, as they can't seem to stick with it over time. He has been very discouraged and disappointed with the results. Very few people have remained smoke-free using this education, this insight or behavioral approach. We discussed the situation, and I told him that his results didn't surprise me if the people he was working with were truly psychologically addicted, because his approach, being so ego-based, wouldn't work with that population based on my understanding of the nature of true addiction. The ego-based approach would only be effective with those who were abusing tobacco, not with those who were addicted to it. The ego-based educational approach to stopping smoking does not take into consideration the necessity of neutralizing the Archetypal Shadow/Archetypal Evil aspect of addiction, which must be accomplished through ego surrender, acknowledgment of powerlessness, and turning to a higher spiritual power. This is the Twelve Steps approach that Smokers Anonymous is taking with people who are psychologically addicted to tobacco.

Interestingly, in the same vein, some recent studies of the effectiveness of different treatment approaches to alcoholism and addiction that have supposedly found that A.A. is statistically no more effective than other approaches (such as rational/emotive, cognitive, behavior modification, etc.) don't make the crucial diagnostic distinction between "abuse" (which can be effectively impacted through other ego-insight-oriented psychotherapy approaches) and "addiction" (which must first put the contaminated, hijacked, compromised ego out of commission before ego-insight approaches can be effective). They unknowingly regard apples and oranges as the same thing. These studies lump "abuse" and "addiction" together in the same category, and miss the all-important significance of their differences, as well as the differences in what is effective treatment for each of the different phenomena. In recent years, our society's get-tough, "zero tolerance" mentality toward everything has not helped. It has resulted in a lumping together of many very important differences and distinctions in many areas, including the differences between experimentation, recreational use, abuse, and addiction itself. Studies that focus on broad definitions of "problem drinkers" and do not make those important diagnostic distinctions are not valid or helpful in understanding alcoholism.

A.A. does also utilize an ego-insight approach in its Steps Four through Ten (in helping addicted individuals to discern and become more conscious of their motivations and behaviors, past and present—the inventory; taking psychological, moral, and ethical responsibility for their actions; and confessing their wrongs and making amends to others), but this is possible only after Steps One, Two, and Three have effectively neutralized the Archetypal Shadow/Archetypal Evil aspect of the addiction.

Also, many current alternative therapeutic approaches to alcoholism and addiction have borrowed heavily from A.A.'s experience and Twelve Step methodology in forming their programs. This raises the question of how much these alternative programs are really substantively different from A.A. at heart. Another potentially distorting variable in these studies is the ubiquity of court-mandated attendances at A.A. and N.A. meetings by people who are forced to be there because of D.W.I. or D.U.I. arrests. A.A. was never meant to be mandated to anyone; it was designed to be voluntary, to draw by attraction and through the natural process of people "hitting bottom" and surrendering. Many, or at least some, of those attending A.A. and N.A. meetings through court mandate have no "desire to quit drinking" or using, which is the one and only requirement A.A./N.A. asks of those participating in their programs.

Let me clarify: I am not saying that the Twelve Steps of A.A. are the only effective way, the only possible treatment program, to deal with alcoholism and addiction. What I am saying is that any approach that does not use the same fundamental psychodynamic principles embodied in the Twelve Steps of A.A. (ego collapse, neutralizing of Archetypal Shadow/Archetypal Evil, conversion experience, ego-Self axis alignment, community, persona/personal shadow work, personal inventory, amends, and helping others, etc.) is doomed to be ineffective and fail. If you remove all of the key ingredients from a medication that has proven to be effective in arresting a life-threatening, incurable disease, it is not reasonable to expect it to do the job.

The alcoholism addiction treatment landscape is scattered with the abandoned wreckage of these grand treatment alternative approaches that have not worked, for many years before and after A.A. This of course does not prevent the newest kid on the block from coming up with the next panacea, claiming superior effectiveness in treating alcoholism and addiction. Many claims have been made that have not held up. The problem is not that naïve, well-meaning folks, as well as charlatans, take people's money and waste their time and energy on things that don't work. It is the fact that alcoholic and addicted individuals die every time a bogus treatment approach knowingly or unknowingly colludes with the Addiction-Shadow-Complex

in enabling the alcoholic or addicted individual to continue participating in his or her addictive behavior. Telling alcoholic addicted people
you can teach them to drink or use socially and moderately is not only
a lie, it hastens their death. A.A. always cautions its members about
looking for a softer, easier way—it knows this territory of false promises very well.

I do believe that, if new treatment approaches emerge that employ these core psychodynamic principles embodied in the Twelve
Steps of A.A., they will be effective. Remember—it's the phenomenon
of addiction and effective treatment I'm concerned about, not the labeling, the club, or the packaging. That being said, it doesn't make a
lot of sense to me to reinvent the wheel when we already have a good
one in A.A. that is available, accessible, user-friendly, works well, and
is free. I am one of those people who believe: "If it ain't broke, don't
fix it."

Ernest Kurtz, in his excellent book on the history of A.A., refers
to the essence of the first three steps of A.A. being the profound realization by the alcoholic that he or she is not God—which is actually
the title of his book: *Not God*. I realize sometimes I am arguing that
the addiction claims to be "God" in the psyche, and at other times
that the alcoholic or addicted individual is making the same inflated
claim for him or herself. Early in the process, the normal, healthy ego
is tempted by inflation to identify with and to believe it is the overly
idealized persona or false self. Later in the process, once the powerful
archetypal energies of the addiction are activated, the person operates
with the addiction as its god—but also, the addiction can now dupe
and delude the person through its possession to a grandiose ego position that falsely believes it, the ego, is god and can control everything,
when in fact it controls nothing and the addiction is really calling all
the shots. I'm trying to describe the phenomenon as I understand it
and have had experience with it. I apologize if in my attempt to describe these things I might confuse or seem to contradict, but it is a
very complicated phenomenon and often doesn't fit into any neat and
tidy or clear categories.

I believe that initially what happens is that the ego overidentifies
with the persona, the false self or fabricated image of oneself. As the
addiction process progresses, the personal shadow gets involved, and
then the potentially addictive behavior comes into play to alleviate

the stress, tension, and conflict in the psychic system. At some point, usually after all the previous dynamics have played out, the potentially addictive behavior is incorporated and subsumed into the Archetypal Shadow/Archetypal Evil component, which is now fully activated, and the person has crossed over from abuse to addiction, and from normal ego-control ability to no ego-control ability as the Addiction-Shadow-Complex takes over the psyche and rules it completely.

Linda Leonard, in her book on addiction and creativity, addresses this first part of the recovery process. She says of Step One of A.A.: "Driven to the bottom by their addiction, they face a humiliation that can be transformed only through humility, through accepting that they are no longer in control or the masters of their own being."[2] In relation to Step Two of A.A., she says that "the addiction can ... serve to bring humans to the consciousness that they are out of relationship to the higher powers of creation."[3] Leonard argues that addiction is about the wrong alignments of human beings with the wrong powers and that healing and recovery (and creativity as part of this) is about the right alignments with the right powers of the universe. It is about taking a leap of faith, which seems absurd; it goes beyond all logic and reason. Kierkegaard says that "it takes humility to take a leap of faith, for the leap is beyond rational control."[4] Giving up ego control is the biggest leap of faith I can imagine.

It is this openness on the part of the recovering alcoholic in Step Two which reaches out to archetypal, transpersonal powers, beyond oneself, perhaps unnamed and unknown, which have the potential to realign one's psyche away from possession and toward a life-giving, life-saving principle. It can truly be a realignment of one's stars, one's fate, one's destiny.

This power greater than ourselves could be God or the A.A. community or the Twelve Steps or even just the possibility that something bigger and greater than us could help us. What is crucial is that we admit we don't have the answers, that we can't figure it out and that we can't control it. This small, yet gigantic step, this shift in attitude consciousness does two things; it opens us to a non-ego solution possibility and it calls upon transpersonal powers or grace to help us in the process.

The ego in service to the Self does not serve itself. The ego trying to truly serve God does not serve the Devil. The ego trying to do the will of God is constantly countering the pitfalls of egotism and choosing against Archetypal Shadow. Bob Dylan had a song with the constant recurring refrain, "you gotta serve somebody" which enumerates all the people and things we can serve, but the point of his song is that we all have to serve something and somebody somehow, so we need to make a conscious choice of who or what it's "gonna be."

B. Shadow Work: Steps Four through Ten of A.A and Stage Four of the Psychodynamics of Recovery

Once the conscious ego has aligned with the true Self and the cork is back in the bottle, so to speak; that is, once Steps One, Two, and Three in A.A have been taken—the ego has recognized the Addiction-Shadow-Complex, disidentified with the false self, and subordinated itself to the higher spiritual power (Self, God, H.P., etc.), which has resulted in the cessation of the addictive behavior (being sober, clean, abstinent, etc.)—then the psychodynamically hard, difficult work of facing and integrating the personal shadow begins. (Remember that Archetypal Shadow/Archetypal Evil can only be checked and neutralized; it cannot be cured, integrated, or eliminated, at least not by human beings.)

Steps Four through Ten of A.A. can all be considered personal shadow work from a Jungian perspective. (On the chart on page 98 it is designated by the grouping of the steps and stages categories under the letter "B.") In the process of individuation, becoming conscious of, accepting and integrating and taking psychological responsibility for our own personal shadows is a major piece of what is worked on for a long time in Jungian analysis.

In A.A., Step Four reads: "Made a searching and fearless moral inventory of ourselves." A.A encourages a person to take a long, honest reflective look at oneself, to face what A.A. calls "character defects," one's failures and weaknesses that have damaged and hurt oneself and others. This requires courage, because this is not easy, so it needs to be fearless and it should be thorough, with no minimizing, rationalizing, or evading of the truth. Therefore it should be a searching inventory, and the moral aspect of the inventory is that one take responsibility for the consequences and effects of his or her choices, decisions, and actions—without excuses.

Note that the moral inventory is of ourselves and not of others, as tempting as that might be. A.A. frowns upon and cautions against what they call "taking other people's inventory," because it is fruitless, often judgmental, and ultimately has nothing to do with one's own sobriety and serenity. The inventory also includes an honest assessment of one's strengths, positive attributes, and good qualities, without exaggeration or devaluing. It is the truth—whatever it is, positive or negative—that sets us free. The inventory also has the benefit of working against pride and inflation, as well as the temptation to start overidentifying once again, in self-righteousness, with an over-idealized persona. Inventory and personal shadow work reinforce humility.

The A.A. book *Twelve Steps and Twelve Traditions* recommends that one examine the Seven Deadly Sins of pride, greed, lust, anger, gluttony, envy, and sloth for starters in taking one's inventory.[5]

Bill W. saw the addiction as turning the natural instincts for sex, relationship, and security, as well as the normal human desire for money, romance, companionship, and prestige into destructive, distorted drives. He felt that the distortion occurred because of "demand." He said: "We have been making unreasonable demands upon ourselves, upon others and upon God. ... Either we ... tried to play God and dominate those about us or we ... insisted on being over-dependent on them."[6]

Remember our definition of the personal shadow: it is the "hidden unconscious aspects of [ourselves], both good and bad which the ego has either repressed or never recognized."[7] It is all the incompatible thoughts, feelings, desires, fantasies, and actions that we have suppressed or repressed into the personal unconscious, along with our more primitive undifferentiated impulses and instincts. Just add our human tendency to power, inflation, and dependency, and this description of the personal shadow is very close to Bill W.'s view of the distorted instincts in alcoholism.

Step Five in A.A. reads: "Admitted to God, to ourselves, and to another human being the exact nature of our wrongs." After the inventory, Step Four, comes confession, which we are told is good for the soul. For those in recovery, Step Five continues the path toward psychological honesty and true humility. When we have to tell not only ourselves, but God and another human being, about our deepest, darkest, most embarrassing, shameful, and humiliating secrets it is not an easy task. Remember those bastard children we had locked up in those closets, attics, and basements of our psyches—well, now it's time that they came out and saw the light of day.

Exploring, owning, and sharing our personal shadow is much of what goes on initially in Jungian analysis. As in A.A., the unburdening of these painful truths about ourselves to another person is a healing and freeing experience, just as it is when one goes to confession (the Sacrament of Reconciliation in Christian tradition) with a good confessor or spiritual director. To no longer have to hide and carry around that shameful bag of sins and failings and humanness is a great relief. Just to have someone else know lightens the load, because we are no longer isolated and alone; we have shared it with another person. Of course it is important to choose a good listener, someone compassionate and understanding who will not judge and condemn us; someone who knows the pain of being human, of being a wonderfully flawed creation.

The Jungian analyst John Sanford, in his book *Healing and Wholeness*, writes about this personal shadow work from the perspective of the healing rites of Asklepius (his spelling of Aesculapius), the Greek god of healing and medicine. Sanford says:

> Once the individual arrived at the temple [of Asklepius], we saw that he had to undergo rites of confession and purification. Until one is right with oneself and one's neighbors, the healing powers of the soul cannot be put into effect. It was at the moment of arrival that the priests at the temple required the supplicant to make amends for his sins before entering the inner sanctum to petition the god of healing. In the language of depth psychology [another term for Jungian Psychology], we call this 'dealing with the shadow,' the inferior, unwanted part of our life and personality. Until one is willing to face one's shadow, the dark side of one's life, the unconscious simply does not open up, and the forces of healing are locked within.
>
> Of course the supplicant knew a confession and purification would be required of him, and we can imagine that on his journey to the temple he was engaged in taking what Alcoholics Anonymous calls his 'personal inventory.' He knew that he would be expected to make his life right, to set his house in order and while this is a painful task, he was driven to it by the greater

pain of his illness. This is also part of the reason wholeness is not possible without pain, for there is great resistance to seeing our shadow; few face their darkness without being driven to it by a greater pain. Yet without this self examination, little or nothing happens.[8]

One of my observations of many of the alcoholics I know is that they'd rather take a bullet to the chest than to have to suffer emotional and psychological pain.

Eckhart Tolle, in his book *The Power of Now*, echoes this observation when he says: "Every addiction arises from an unconscious refusal to face and move through your own pain. Every addiction starts with pain and ends with pain. Whatever the substance you are addicted to—alcohol, food, legal or illegal drugs, or a person—you are using something or somebody to cover up your pain."[9] Steps Four and Five force recovering alcoholics to deal with emotional and psychological pain without the numbing escape mechanism of their addictions.

When you make a moral and fearless inventory, confront and psychologically own your personal shadow (Step Four), and then have to go through the often embarrassing, humiliating, and shameful acknowledgment and sharing of that inventory with God and another person (Step Five), it puts you right smack in the middle of significant suffering of your emotional and psychological pain, especially knowing and facing the pain and suffering and hardships you have inflicted upon others in your life.

Steps Four and Five do not allow for denial, minimizing, rationalization, evasion, or excuses, and you can't just keep it to yourself as a secret. These steps involve a level of ruthless self-honesty that most alcoholics and addicted individuals are unaccustomed to. A.A. sponsors are especially helpful in guiding individuals through these steps. It should also be noted that inventory is not just about failures, bad or unacceptable qualities in a person, but also includes positive attributes, talents, and gifts. Often our personal shadow contains unclaimed instinctual, positive, and creative aspects that have been repressed, devalued, or denied. They too belong on the list. The inventory and sharing of it are not meant to lower self-esteem, self-concept, or self-worth; they are meant to help us see ourselves more objectively, honestly, and truthfully as we are. Since the Addiction-Shadow-Complex traffics in deception, dishonesty, and lies, it does not like it when we traffic in the truth or what really is. An honest inventory reduces some of the potential avenues the addiction can take to try to manipulate us for its purpose.

For those wanting a better, more in-depth understanding of the Twelve Steps of A.A., I greatly recommend the A.A. book *Twelve Steps and Twelve Traditions* as the best, clearest, most readable explanation of the Twelve Steps, how they work and why we take them.

Marion Woodman encourages addicted individuals to take up and bear the cross of their inventory and confession so that transformation may occur. She says: "By contacting that energy in a numinous experience of suffering, dying and then rising again, the ego sacrifices itself to a Higher Power, is enlarged and transformed so that it returns to ordinary life with a new outlook."[10]

With all of the meaningless, senseless, chaotic suffering that the addicted individual has gone through and inflicted on others while using, it is a gigantic leap of faith to believe that now self-embraced suffering and pain can have inherent meaning and redemptive value in one's recovery process.

Bill W., in his first published Christmas card, hails with "Greeting to All Members," and affirms this necessary principle of suffering in his own eloquent way when he says, "Nor can men and women of A.A. ever forget that only through suffering did they find enough humility to enter the portals of that New World. How privileged we are to understand so well the divine paradox that strength rises from weakness, that humiliation goes before resurrection: that pain is not only the price, but the very touchstone of spiritual rebirth."[11]

A.A. Steps Six and Seven can be seen as a continuation of the process of integrating personal shadow work by placing these defects of character in the hands of a Higher Power (God) and asking him to heal and remove them if that is his will. Step Six reads: "Were entirely ready to have God remove all these defects of character," and Step Seven reads: "Humbly asked Him to remove our shortcomings." The readiness of a person recovering from addiction to place everything in the hands of the higher spiritual power and to rely on transcendent grace, not personal ego, to be transformed, follows the best of all the great spiritual traditions. Steps Six and Seven continue to emphasize the humbling of the ego, which makes it much harder for the Addiction-

Shadow-Complex to get back in control of the recovering individual. These steps are like inoculations that protect us and prevent us from getting reinfected by the potentially fatal disease.

In psychodynamic terms, we bring all our personal shadow work to the Self, to comment on, to integrate, and to transform. We keep open to the promptings from the Self in our dreams, relationships, experiences, and synchronicities to teach us what we need to learn about becoming spiritually whole. Information from one's dreams and from the unconscious is essential in getting honest and truly knowing oneself, especially the nature of one's persona and personal shadow.

A.A. says that Steps Eight and Nine are about putting the faith of Steps Six and Seven into action: "Faith without works is dead." Steps Eight and Nine are the works that keep the faith alive. Step Eight of A.A. reads: "Made a list of all persons we had harmed, and became willing to make amends to them all." Step Eight emphasizes "the willingness" to make amends to "all," so we are not tempted to minimize, cut short our list, or begin "crayfishing" (backing out) before anything has been truly explored and owned. We must continue our ruthless honesty in assessing the list of the people we have hurt or harmed. We cannot apologize or make amends if the specific nature of our offenses against others is not clearly known and understood—more painful shadow work to do!

Step Nine reads: "Made direct amends to such people wherever possible, except when to do so would injure them or others." Generalizations and global generic apologies are not what Steps Eight and Nine are all about. The intention is not to comfort ourselves and feel good about forgiveness or absolution. These steps are about paying back debts we owe—financially, emotionally, relationally, and spiritually; about fixing things we have broken or neglected; about righting the wrongs of our lives toward others. If that results in us feeling better in the end, that's fine, but that is not the goal or primary purpose of these steps.

Take note that Step Nine instructs, "direct amends"—indirect amends are not being advocated here; asking a friend to apologize for us won't cut it. Which people we go to, of those on our list we have harmed, should have nothing to do with whether they are willing or able to forgive us. Just going to safe people on the list who we are confident will be understanding and forgiving misses the main point once again—these steps are not about me and my comfort; they are about my concern and commitment to the well-being of others I have injured or hurt in some way. Steps Eight and Nine are concrete, operationalizing actions of the Golden Rule principle of treating ourselves and others as we would like to be treated (Love thy neighbor as thyself).

Once again, these steps are rooted in ego humility, in selflessness, in honesty, and in taking personal psychological, social, and moral responsibility for our behaviors and their effects on others. Some people might say Steps Eight and Nine are about righting our karma or about cultivating the Buddhist understanding of right thoughts and right actions. When we have a history of broken promises, of disappointing, hurting, and betraying others, of lying, cheating, and stealing, especially for the sake of our addiction, the Addiction-Shadow-Complex would love us to minimize, rationalize, ignore, deny, and forget the destructive wake left behind from our actions and behaviors, because real conscience and real guilt are deadly to the addiction.

Steps Eight and Nine are about taking moral responsibility for our past and wanting to set it right. Steps Eight and Nine are about taking action, not just having good intentions which we know pave the road to hell.

Linda Leonard comments on Step Nine and making amends: "To *amend* means to grow or become better by reforming oneself, by improving one's life, thus acknowledging authentic guilt, the debt of existence that we owe our Creator."[12]

In the Roman Catholic Church tradition, an essential component and condition for forgiveness from God or the absolution of our sins in what is known as the Holy Sacrament of Reconciliation (more commonly known as going to confession) is that a person must make amends, substantive restitution, for the sins and offenses one has committed against others. The sacrament obligates one to rectify the wrong through some action, if possible, or else the forgiveness is not granted by God through his priest-representative. One must also be firmly committed to change one's behavior and "to sin no more," that is, to mend and repair by action and not just intention. The priest will often require what is known as a penance, a specific restitution or righting of the wrong committed against others, and these penances involve the doing of something very direct by the person asking forgiveness. Examples of such penances are: paying back stolen property or money, direct apologies, volunteering to help others, replacing broken objects, saying only nice things for five days, giving to the poor, refraining from criticism, visiting people in need, praying for an enemy, donations to charity, an anonymous act of kindness, offering the olive branch first, and of course saying three Our Fathers and three Hail Mary's, etc.

One of the psychologically helpful aspects of Steps Eight and Nine is that it directly attacks the self-referencing narcissism of the addicted person and provides a direct and powerful opportunity to put others before oneself in thought, feeling, and action. Even the proviso in Step Nine that one should not try to make amends when it will hurt or injure others demands that one operate thoughtfully and considerately toward others' well-being, not just in the mechanical way of obligation. For some this is a completely new experience and way of relating to other human beings.

In Jungian terms, integrating the personal shadow or doing shadow work involves much more than just a theoretical awareness of things. It is not just abstract intellectualizing. It involves more than insight and understanding. We must learn to eat our shadow, so to speak—to digest it, to break it down, assimilate it, and integrate it into the cells of our bodies, our spirits and souls. This involves the moral imperative to change the way we treat ourselves and others through the way we live and act and think and feel. We cannot truly own and accept our shadow without it making us kinder, fairer, more compassionate, forgiving, merciful, and less judgmental of others and of ourselves.

Jung actually viewed the personal shadow as synonymous with the Christian concept of "original sin,"[13] which we are all given by virtue of being human and must struggle to own, become conscious of, and redeem through the Self (or through Christ in the Christian tradition or the Higher Power in A.A.).

The Jungian analyst Jolande Jacobi, in her book *The Way of Individuation*, echoes and amplifies these thoughts about shadow integration and A.A. Steps Four through Ten when she says:

> The concept of integration involves more than a mere knowledge of the [personal] shadow's qualities. For example an alcoholic in order to be cured [perhaps the wrong term to use], must

not only be conscious of his tendency or compulsion to drink—which many of them deny—but must also discover the deeper reasons that have induced his craving. These reasons are always shadow qualities which he cannot accept, which he flees from in order to rid himself of the pangs of conscience their recognition would entail. The precondition for a cure [I prefer recovery], therefore, is that the alcoholic should keep these shadow qualities constantly before him, seeing in his mind's eye this drinker in himself as his unswerving companion, until he can no longer forget his presence. For "a content can be integrated only when its double aspect has become conscious and when it is grasped not merely intellectually but understood according to its feeling value" (*Aion*, CW, Vol. 9, Part II, p. 30).[14]

It may seem strange, but one of the greatest danger points for alcoholic and addicted individuals to relapse and return to the living hell of their addiction is that they forget that they are still alcoholic and addicted; things get going so well sometimes that they begin to believe that perhaps now they can have that drink or drug or sexual encounter or play a slot machine and still remain in control. This ego inflation, self-permission deception is all the opportunity the Addiction-Shadow-Complex needs to re-hijack the ego system and re-control the psyche. A.A. cautions that health, wealth, and intelligence can be the biggest dangers to sobriety. They can make it easy to forget that one is still an alcoholic. This is one of the helpful psychological reasons why at A.A. and other Twelve Step meetings people always introduce themselves by their first name and then name what their addiction is; for example, "Hi, my name is Tim. I am an alcoholic." Or "Hi, my name is Ann. I'm addicted to alcohol, drugs, and sex." This is not done masochistically or punitively; it is not superfluous. It is not done to limit one's identity to being only alcoholic or addicted, nor is it done to diminish or devalue the person or their self-worth or self-esteem in any way. It is done so that the person continually reminds him or herself and others that he or she is addicted, and that it is crucial that one *never* forget this fact, because forgetting it puts in peril one's sobriety and one's very life.

Once one is touched by Archetypal Shadow/Archetypal Evil, the contamination, like radiation, creates a permanent vulnerability, which is very dangerous and should never be forgotten. One should always be on guard against physical or psychological re-exposure. Owning the addiction in a direct and personal way at A.A. and Twelve Step meetings is a kind of collective and self ritual inoculation against the ever-present dangers of the cunning and manipulative addiction, by this remembering, not forgetting, and affirming it out loud for one-self and for everyone else.

This is also the reason that A.A. is seemingly fanatical about its advice that, once sober, the addict must try never to take the first drink, because for alcoholics it opens the door to the rest of the addiction and to the overwhelmingly murderous energies of Archetypal Shadow/ Archetypal Evil. This position taken by A.A. is not about overkill or some unexamined puritanical streak in the program; it is based on the practical, hard-won experience and price paid by many who were so-ber and doing well, but took the first drink and were lost forever in the black hole of the Addiction-Shadow-Complex—they paid for that first drink with their lives.

The anonymous aspect of A.A. and its tradition of using only first names is done not only to protect the alcoholic, addicted person from the condemnation and judgment of others in society, but also as a self-protection, so that the person is not tempted to make his or her re-covery into an inflated-persona ego trip, where he or she becomes the poster child winning the national award for being the most outstand-ing recovering alcoholic or addict in the country. Anonymity also protects people from themselves and from the dangers of that inflated ego, which can open the door to reactivate the addiction.

How important it is to stay conscious of the addiction as one's perpetual "unswerving companion"! The "feeling value" referred to in Jacobi's quote of Jung does not refer to emotions or affects. The trans-lation of this term in English is very confusing, and I wish we had another, easier word or phrase to better describe and clarify the psy-chological phenomenon to which Jung refers. What Jung means by "feeling value" is more about the conscious, reflective, thoughtful val-ues we embrace in our lives, which influence and guide our decisions, choices, and behaviors—the values by which we truly live our lives. Jung is saying in this quote that for something to be integrated psy-chologically we must become conscious of its "double aspect"—of its shadow, of what is constructive and destructive, helpful and damag-ing about it—and then we must apply this conscious awareness to our values and how we live our lives. If we apply this idea to dealing with addiction dynamics, it is a great prescription for discernment, becoming more conscious and transforming toward wholeness.

Step Ten in A.A. reads: "Continued to take personal inventory, and when we were wrong promptly admitted it." Step Ten moves our shadow work from focusing on our history and past manifestations of personal shadow and begins applying it through the continuation of our taking our personal inventory into the present as a normative process in the way we live our lives, and into the future. It encourages continued examination of our thoughts, motives, and actions. It encourages us to continue to try to stay conscious, especially with an eye toward ever-present shadow issues and how they affect our dealings with other people. When we go unconscious and hurt others because of our personal shadow, we admit it "promptly," take responsibility, own it and make amends.

Jung's assertion that for something to be integrated into the psyche it must be consciously wrestled with in its positive and negative implications (its double aspect) and then it must take hold in making a difference in how we live our lives (its feeling value) is the essence of Steps Four through Ten of A.A.: making a moral inventory; admitting the exact nature of our wrongs to ourselves, to God, and to another human being; being ready to have God remove our defects of character and asking him to do so; making a list of all persons harmed and making amends to them when appropriate; and finally to keep practicing these steps for the rest of our lives. Wow, what a way to live!

The importance of confronting and integrating the personal shadow in the addiction recovery process cannot be overemphasized. It literally takes up over half (seven) of the Twelve Steps of A.A. In addition to all the reasons already stated of why this shadow work is so crucial, there is one more that has been alluded to previously but not spelled out directly, and this is that the wounding aspect of both the personal shadow and of Archetypal Shadow/Archetypal Evil sets into motion the Wounded Healer archetype, which may be the ultimate key to the transpersonal energy and grace necessary for healing and recovery from addiction. We can see the Wounded Healer motif previously touched on in the fact that the best A.A. sponsors have been to hell and back, in the comments by Marion Woodman about the numinous experience of suffering being redemptive, in Bill W.'s Christmas card about pain being the touchstone of rebirth, and in the section on how integrating personal shadow makes us better and more compassionate human beings. We can even make a case for the fact that Archetypal Shadow/Archetypal Evil, for the alcoholic or addicted person, is the impetus for the search for Archetypal Spiritual Good (God, the Higher Power, the Self, etc.), without which all is lost. So even the horror and terribleness of Archetypal Shadow/Archetypal Evil has a potentially positive aspect through its wounding, in that it drives and motivates the person, like nothing else, to find a way to not die sacrificed on the altar of addiction.

Awareness of the Wounded Healer archetype can be very helpful—to understand this great, long-standing, mysterious archetype, how it is universal, and how it has emerged again and again at every time in history, from Shamans through Asklepius, the Greek god of healing referred to by John Sanford, to Jesus, the Christ, who redeemed the world through his suffering, death, and resurrection.

Acceptance of personal wounding, suffering, and pain as an essential, meaningful prerequisite for healing and transformation and redemption, as well as for the benefit of others, is what the real payoff is for integrating the personal shadow and finding the proper ego attitude to deal with and neutralize Archetypal Shadow/Archetypal Evil by turning to the great, powerful, positive reservoirs of Archetypal Spiritual Goodness and Light (the Higher Power, God, the Self, etc.).

If a recovering alcoholic or addicted individual can see themselves not as an isolated, alienated, lonely individual caught in useless, meaningless suffering, but as a specially chosen one, as a co-wounded healer in union with all the great (but always humble) wounded healers of human history, it can make all the difference in being saved and perhaps helping save the world, or at least a part of it.

I always suspect, when I've heard someone who I know has suffered greatly, refer to themselves with a slight knowing smile as a "grateful alcoholic," that they have gained a true appreciation for the wounded healer from the inside out. I think it is a statement of true humility and great honesty.

C. STAYING IN THE LIGHT: A.A. STEPS ELEVEN AND TWELVE AND STAGES FIVE AND SIX OF THE PSYCHODYNAMICS OF RECOVERY

Step Eleven of A.A. reads: "Sought through prayer and meditation to improve our conscious contact with God as we understood Him, praying only for knowledge of His will for us and the power to carry that out."

Step Twelve reads: "Having had a spiritual awakening as the result of these steps, we tried to carry this message to alcoholics, and to practice these principles in all our affairs."

In the psychodynamics of recovery this is Stage Five, "Ongoing Maintenance of the Ego-Self Axis," and Stage Six, "Living in Service with the Self." (On the chart on page 98 it is designated by the grouping under the letter "C".)

These two steps of A.A. and stages of recovery go hand in hand. Jung often remarked that the greater one's consciousness, the greater is one's responsibility psychologically to oneself, to others, to the world, and to God. Step Eleven of A.A. can be translated in Jungian terms as the need to continue to nurture, maintain, and protect a strong, vital ego connection with the Self, that is, to keep the Ego-Self axis open and functioning and working properly. This is the ongoing process of personal analysis and our ongoing journey in light of the Self. This is about the discernment and self-reflection of prayer and meditation toward knowing and doing the will of God. In Jungian terms, it is actively and consciously living out our individuation.

Linda Leonard says that Step Eleven of A.A. "allows us to dwell in this silent spring of life. ... to be a channel for the creative process. ... [and attend to] being in the moment."[15]

Step Eleven reinforces and helps operationalize the A.A. slogans "Let go and let God," "Easy does it," and "One day at a time." To "let go and let God," we have to be willing to give up our ego agendas and cultivate a desire to do the will of God and to turn over the ultimate control to him. To know the will of God, we must pray and meditate and reflect, as well as listen to our bodies, our emotions, our thoughts, our intuitions, our dreams, our deepest values, and to what the universe sends us through other people and through synchronicities. Once we have discerned God's will in our life, then we can pray for courage and strength to carry it out. "Easy does it" reminds us that we don't have to have all of the answers all of the time—in fact, not even most of the time—so we can relax and trust that if we put ourselves in the hands of God, no matter what happens God will help us get through it, including sickness, suffering, and death. Finally, "One day at a time" reminds us to stay in the now, not to try to bite off more than we can chew, not to worry about the past or the future, which we can't do anything about. "One day at a time" is not only about sobriety, but about being more present to the present, more alive to the fullness of this moment today.

Step Eleven of A.A. leads directly to Step Twelve. If all we have learned is not put into service for others, to somehow make the world a better place, then it is useless. Step Twelve calls upon recovering alcoholics and addicts to bring their faith, hope, strength, and experience to others suffering from addiction, and to practice the principles of their spiritual awakening in all areas of their lives. Once again, Linda Leonard comments beautifully on Step Twelve: "Without this creative transformation there would be no gifts given or received. This energy of creative love through spiritually transformative giving is the very same that happens through the twelfth step, the act of gratitude and giving through which a person shares experience, strength, and hope with others. This helps enable the process of recovery from addiction."[16]

Jung believed that one of the benefits of the individuation process is that it makes for better citizens of the world. The more of our own evil and personal shadow we can contain and transform in our own process, the less gets projected onto others and into the world. The more authentically we are living our unique destiny, the more we have in common and the more we are connected with all of humanity. The more conscious we are, the greater is our responsibility to our fellow human beings and to all creation.

The Twelve Steps of A.A. allow the opportunity and the chance for alcoholic and addicted individuals to embark on their unique path and spiritual destiny; they allow for alcoholic and addicted individuals to participate in the individuation process.

Two final comments on A.A. and the Twelve Steps. The entire A.A. program is geared toward sobriety, healing, and recovery through relationships both human and spiritual (the fellowship of other recovering alcoholics, sponsors, and the Higher Power). A.A. is about community. It is about bringing the addicted individual out of the lonely, torturous isolation of the Addiction-Shadow-Complex into the loving, caring, compassionate community, especially of those who truly understand and know.

All of the Twelve Steps are written in plural form—"we, our, us"—not once is "I, me, or my" used, the point simply being that one is never alone in the recovery process and this should never be forgotten. A.A. is about a community of support, of fellowship, not about a "pull yourself up by your own bootstraps" individualism.

A question I haven't yet addressed is what happens psychodynamically in the recovery process, to the ego that has previously been completely controlled and dominated by the Addiction-Shadow-Complex, after it has surrendered and put itself out of commission through the first step of A.A. Jung reminds us that we must have a functioning ego to operate psychologically, that is, we must have an ego to process and integrate, to register feelings and information from the unconscious, as well as to focus, think, make decisions and judgments and take action.

The ego continues to exist after taking Step One, but the detoxification from the Addiction-Shadow-Complex takes time, as well as sobriety and abstinence. Once the Archetypal Shadow/Archetypal Evil is neutralized by the Higher Power, the ego begins to align away from the Archetypal Shadow/Archetypal Evil toward the Higher Power or true Self. This allows the ego to begin to have a chance to return to a normal, healthy role as the central organ of consciousness in the psyche. But initially, it is so weak and confused and abused by the Addiction-Shadow-Complex, which has so thoroughly dominated and controlled it, that it cannot rely upon itself to do the job it is meant to do, so it must initially rely upon an ego-surrogate support system of sponsors, recovering peers, A.A. meetings, program readings, working the Twelve Steps, and transpersonal grace from the Higher Power or Self.

My observation is that gradually the ego detoxifies, strengthens, and returns in most cases to its normal, healthy role in the psyche. In a study referred to by *The Harvard Medical School Mental Health Letter*, the findings support such a conclusion:

> Studies suggest that serious tension, depression, feelings of inadequacy and personality disorders often persist [after sobriety has begun, but] ... that abstinence does make a big difference,

> but only after a long time, as much as two or three years. ... [Stopping drinking] for many months is no guarantee of recovery. One long term study found that alcoholics who had not had a drink in ten years were hardly distinguishable from people who had never been alcoholic at all; those who had been abstinent for less than three years had most of the same psychological and social problems as active alcoholics [they were, however, less likely to die of illness caused by alcohol].[17]

Once again, the practical, firsthand experience of A.A. has operated with this knowledge and understanding for many years, in that it advises newly recovering alcoholics and addicts to not make any major life decisions or changes in the first year of sobriety. Obviously one's judgment, assessment, and perceptions of things (the ego's normal job) is still shaky and not to be trusted. There is also, by sponsors, an informal referring to people who have only been in recovery one or two years as "babies," because it takes time to recover, to get the program, to learn how to walk the walk, to strengthen and heal. The insanity of addiction does not leave overnight because a person has stopped the addictive behavior.

The good news is that over time, ten years or more, the ego functioning of sober, recovering alcoholic and addicted individuals is indistinguishable from the healthy, normal ego functioning of nonalcoholic, nonaddicted individuals.

So the ego does seem to be able, under the right conditions and circumstances (sobriety and recovery), to overcome in time the terrible, destructive, and devastating effects of the addiction and to return to its appropriate, healthy role and function in the psyche, as long as the addiction is not reactivated and the Addiction-Shadow-Complex is not allowed to hijack the ego system and consciousness once again.

The healing process of recovery in A.A. through the Twelve Steps has mapped out and operationalized Jung's observations in his letter to Bill W. that what he calls a "higher understanding" (recovery) can happen "by an act of grace" (Steps One, Two, and Three of A.A.) or "through a higher education of the mind beyond the confines of mere rationalism" (working the Twelve Steps of A.A.). Jung understood how crucial grace and community are to resisting the power of evil, and saw clearly that both were in great abundance in the program of Alcoholics Anonymous.

CHAPTER FIVE

"Using Dreams" of Recovering Alcoholic and Addicted Individuals

I have added this chapter to the book in the hope that it will help alcoholic and addicted individuals to appreciate and utilize dreams as an aid in their healing and recovery process. I also believe this material can be helpful to sponsors, addictions counselors, psychoanalysts, and mental health practitioners in general in their work with people in recovery. I believe dreams can be of value in diagnosis, prognosis, and treatment of addiction.

Reed Morrison, a psychologist who specializes in chemical dependency treatment, published an article entitled "Dream Mapping in Chemical Dependency Recovery."[1] In the article, he presents a general theoretical view of certain types of dreams appearing at six progressive stages of recovery, which he believes can be tracked and assessed. He gives these six stages literary and mythological titles. The first stage is "The Dark Night," when the person is still using, that is, actively participating in one's addiction behavior. This stage is characterized by a sense of being lost, divided, and confused. It may be filled with poor sleep and threatening, guilt-ridden dreams that may lead the person to seek help.

Stage two is called "Pandora's Box": this is when the alcoholic or addicted person gets help and treatment and initially gets sober and stops using. The dreams here usually resume with great force, and are characterized by themes of alienation, violence, mutilation, bizarre sexuality, and persecution. Morrison sees the time frame on these dreams to be within the first forty-five days of recovery.

Stage three is called "The Dragon Fight," where the alcoholic or addicted person confronts the denial and rationalization of the addiction. Dreams in this stage, he believes, are about confronting fear, with images of battles and struggles with demons. This stage is about taking ownership of oneself and developing new roles. The time frame is twenty to ninety days in recovery. Obviously, these stages are not precise and clear-cut in terms of overlapping processes and time frames.

Stage four is called "Rebirth." This is the stage where the person feels relief and freedom from the addiction and is on a kind of sobriety-abstinence "high," and dreams about positive movement, new living spaces, acceptance, spiritual presence, rescue, ownership, and positive self-identification.

Stage five is called "The Descent." It is where the person either relapses, goes on a "dry drunk" (meaning that they regress back to old drinking and dysfunctional behaviors while still sober), or gets very discouraged again, feeling like they are slipping back into the abyss. Dreams at this stage are about unfinished business, guilt, and confusion. The estimated time frame on this stage is sixty to one hundred and fifty days in recovery.

Stage six is called "The Return." It is where the person is beginning to integrate and solidify new and positive behaviors in recovery. Dreams here are characterized by images of wholeness, home, and renewal. This stage is from ninety to one hundred and eighty days in recovery.

Morrison then observes a continuous process of confrontation, descent, and reintegration along with their corresponding dreams, which he places under the broad general context of growth and the individuation process.

I find Morrison's dream mapping interesting and encouraging in many ways. It is attempting to link dreams and addiction and the recovery process in a meaningful way. It offers a kind of broad general outline of what the process may look like, and he encourages those in recovery to take their dreams seriously.

On the other hand, I think his map of the phenomena of dreams in the addiction recovery process is too simplistic, overly sequential, and that the time frames of the dreams' occurring feels arbitrarily determined and, I think, unrealistic. There is so much individual variation in dreams and in different people that generalization schemes can be dangerous and not reflective of the complexity and variety of the phenomena and of what is possible. Perhaps if Morrison had mapped and observed more than one person's dream process in recovery before he published his article it would have produced a better, more nuanced, and perhaps more accurate offering to help people better understand how dreams can mirror, inform, and aid in the recovery process.

My focus regarding dreams will be specifically on the phenomenon of the "using dreams" of recovering alcoholic and addicted individuals. It is based on a self-report survey given to patients in treatment at an alcohol/drug treatment facility in Louisiana where I was working over a two-year period in 1990 and 1991. I received 104 responses from patients. Thirty-seven people, or approximately 36%, reported a decrease in their normal ability to recall their dreams once they began abusing either alcohol or drugs. Fifty-seven people (57%) reported having dreams in which they were participating in drinking alcohol or taking drugs, which is the phenomenon I am referring to by the term "using dreams." I also interviewed and discussed the issue of "using dreams" with many individuals and groups with a range of abstinence/sobriety from one day to over forty years, as well as tracking the dreams, using and otherwise, of my recovering alcoholic and addicted clients who were or are in analysis with me. Though my results and assertions are not, strictly speaking, scientific, I do believe they are a fairly accurate reflection or map of the phenomenon of "using dreams" of recovering alcoholic and addicted individuals.

What I found was that, in general, alcohol/drug addicted individuals have poorer recall of their dreams than the normal general population. They seem to have either totally blocked their dreams or to have diminished recall in the quantity and quality of the dream material remembered. Of course, this varies from individual to individual depending upon a number of factors, including the stage and progression of one's addiction, the heaviness of usage as well as the nature of the substance abused, and what one's normal dream recall looks like. Some people, addicted or not, are better at dream recall than others.

Numerous studies have confirmed that most drugs disturb natural sleep patterns and decrease REM (Rapid Eye Movement) time during sleep. Most dreams, not all, occur during REM sleep time.

All of the following drugs have been found to decrease and disturb REM sleep: alcohol, barbiturates, amphetamines, and some antidepressants. My observation is that dream recall is also significantly diminished during initial physical alcohol/drug detoxification and in early recovery. Recall seems to improve significantly by six months into sobriety and abstinence (number of dreams remembered increases as well as the content details of the dreams in general).

The area of dreams related to addiction that has always most interested me personally and professionally has been the "drinking dreams" of alcoholics and the "using dreams" of those addicted to drugs and other substances and behaviors. A "using dream" is any dream where the addicted individual is involved in his or her dream in participating, or being tempted to participate, in his or her addictive behavior. In observing this phenomenon I found that the reaction of the dream ego (that is, the dreamer's subjective ego-reaction in the dream itself), as well as the actual reaction of the waking conscious ego, which is the person's actual, normal waking reaction to "using," are diagnostically and prognostically very significant.

When we sleep, the dream ego is the person or perspective in the dream that we identify as ourselves in the dream, as opposed to other characters or aspects of content in the dream that we don't experience as ours. It is what we hear, see, feel, smell, say, think, touch, imagine, and do in the dream itself. It is the character or aspect of the dream we refer to as "I" when we tell the story of the dream. The waking ego is what we normally identify as the "I" in our everyday waking life, our reactions and experiences and perceptions of things, etc.

The dream ego and the waking ego are not identical; they don't always react or experience or perceive in the same way. Sometimes they are polar opposites. For example, in a dream I might see my best friend executed and my reaction in the dream might be to calmly and unemotionally observe, and nod in consensual agreement. Contrast this with my reaction when I wake up. I am horrified and feel guilty that I tried to do nothing in my dream to stop the execution or to save my friend. Sometimes the reactions of the dream ego and the waking ego are completely congruous, sometimes similar, sometimes different, and sometimes they are so opposite it seems like two different people. Sometimes our dream ego will say and do and feel and not feel things that seem strange and alien, and completely foreign and out of character to our conscious waking ego. This is a great opportunity to look at potential shadow issues, to see and own thoughts, feelings, motives, and actions that we are denying, minimizing, rationalizing, or trying to avoid. These differences are psychologically significant and are to be consciously and reflectively explored.

Traditional wisdom, of a Jungian sort, holds that the dream ego always, in a sense, precedes the conscious waking ego because it already knows something more, is a little bit ahead of the game, has more information because of its access to the unconscious. It often sees and knows things already that the waking ego is unaware of or is just beginning to realize.

I have found a wide range of dream ego and waking ego reactions to drinking and using dreams of alcoholic and addicted individuals, in recovery or not. How long an addicted person has been sober, straight, clean, or not using; what one's attitude toward sobriety and recovery is; as well as whether a person is, as they say in A.A., "working their program" (that means participating actively in recovery, using their support system, going to A.A. meetings, doing the Twelve Steps, reading the Big Book and recovery literature, talking with their sponsors, etc.), all can affect the nature of the dream ego and the waking ego's reactions to drinking or using in a dream.

The reactions of the dream ego and the waking ego seem to move between two primarily opposite poles from a "Feels Great" reaction to drinking or using to a "Feels Awful" reaction to the same. The third possibility is that the reaction falls somewhere in between the "Feels Great"/"Feels Awful" poles. In assessing a using dream it is important to compare and contrast the dream ego with the waking ego's reactions to the using in the dream. (Refer to the diagram on page 132.)

"Feels Great" Using Dream Reactions

Typically, a using dream with a "Feels Great" reaction by the dream ego involves the addicted individual participating in his or her addictive behavior (drinking, drugs, gambling, sex, smoking, food, etc.) in the dream and finding it pleasurable and enjoyable. It is often experienced in the dream as getting high and as if the person is getting away with something, breaking the rules, getting around the system, and not getting caught or having to pay the consequences. The dream

---

"Using Dreams"

The reactions of the Dream Ego and the Waking Ego to addiction use in a dream can be viewed on a four-point scale, ranging from one pole of "Feels Great" to use, to the opposite pole of "Feels Awful" to use.

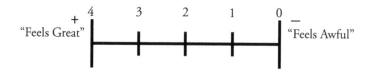

Assess both the Dream Ego's and the Waking Ego's reaction to a Using Dream.

    A. "Feels Great" Using Dream
    B. "Feels Awful" Using Dream
    C. Somewhere-in-between Using Dream

---

ego very much likes and feels good about the using—the "Feels Great" reaction. There is no sense of guilt or fear or anxiety, failure or remorse involved.

When the person awakens from the dream, the waking ego reaction is also very important. If the waking ego reaction is identical to the dream ego reaction—in that it feels great to at least be able to use and get high in one's dream when actual using in external reality is not possible or acceptable at the time—this is a strong indication diagnostically that the person is still very much under the powerful control of the Addiction-Shadow-Complex, and probably has not successfully and effectively taken Steps One, Two, and Three of A.A. The person has not yet had the necessary and essential experience of the relativizing of the ego in relation to the Self (the Higher Power). In A.A. terms, he or she has probably not "hit bottom" yet. Often the individual has been forced or pressured into some sort of sobriety or non-using or treatment program by others (the spouse, the family, the courts, the boss, the EAP, etc.), but at this stage is not really invested in or committed to his or her own recovery process. The motivation at this stage is usually to "get the heat off" oneself so that resumption of the using can continue under the radar when things cool down. The probability of this person relapsing into the addiction is very high as soon as he or she has the chance or the opportunity to do so. The vulnerability is still very high. He or she is still not ready to take the steps necessary to save one's life.

This congruous alignment of dream ego and waking ego as a "Feels Great" reaction to using in a dream usually occurs very early in sobriety and recovery, or else it comes when individuals are very close to or on the verge of, if not already, relapsing into the addiction by actually using again. The dream can be a warning anticipation or actual confirmation of this fact.

This kind of "Feels Great" dream can also be viewed as an unconscious compensation for not being able to use because the addiction is being suppressed and denied satisfaction by the circumstances (being in detox, a treatment facility, or temporarily not having access to the addiction behavior). It is, in a sense, a classic Freudian wish-fulfillment dream with potentially very dangerous consequences.

James Hall, a Jungian analyst, in a book he wrote on Jungian dream interpretation, says of this type of dream: "Non-drinking alcoholics, for example, not infrequently dream of drinking soon after they have ceased to drink in their daily lives. The same type of dream can be observed in cigarette smokers who give up tobacco. Such dreams, simple in structure, suggest that the pattern of ego-identity in which the shadow activity [the addiction behavior] was embedded still persists, although the ego no longer identifies with it. To see these dreams simplistically as wish fulfillment risks miring the ego in past attitudes and behavior patterns, rather than encouraging its movement away from them."[2]

I agree with Hall that interpreting a using dream to justify a reductionistic regression back into addictive behavior does not serve the best interest of the individual and would better be interpreted as a caution, a warning that "there is still danger here," which helps one move toward the light and freedom of recovery in the Self, in the Higher Power.

The diagnostic implications of this kind of "Feels Great" using dream early in recovery is that the ego-identity of the person is still primarily under the psychological domination of the Addiction-Shadow-Complex and its prime directive and desire to continue its power, influence, and control over the person through the person's participation in the addiction behavior. Remember that the Addiction-Shadow-Complex is fed and fueled through the addictive behavior, and when that is cut off, for whatever reason, it goes into a panic-driven survival mode, attempting, demanding at all costs that it be fed and not be slowly starved to death or, perhaps more aptly, not be put in some kind of suspended hibernation. The Addiction-Shadow-Complex uses whatever is available to try to regain control, including using dreams to tempt and try to erode fledgling resolve and barriers to reenactment of the addictive behavior that allows it to actively live on and flourish.

If the Addiction-Shadow-Complex can reactivate the overwhelming craving and obsession with the addictive behavior, it has a chance to get back into the driver's seat and run the show once again, to the destruction of the addicted individual and his or her life. The Addiction-Shadow-Complex is constantly looking for any weakness, any vulnerability, any opening in one's thoughts, feelings, desires, and attitudes; in one's body and physiology; in one's relationships and, yes, in one's dreams to exploit the situation to its advantage.

Recall the study in the *Harvard Medical School Mental Health Letter* I referred to previously, about the continuing psychological and social problems of recovering alcoholics being basically the same as actively using alcoholics for up to three years of abstinence and sobriety. The phenomena in this study are congruous with my observations that most of the "Feels Great" using dreams occur in the first three years of sobriety, when the addicted person's ego and psychological processes are still confused, shaky, and more vulnerable to the persuasions of the Addiction-Shadow-Complex. After three years of sobriety or not participating in one's addictive behavior, the Addiction-Shadow-Complex is much weaker and thinner, and may even dismember to some extent—but remember that it always has the potential, because of the Archetypal Shadow/Archetypal Evil aspect in the addiction, to come back with a vengeance if the circumstances, conditions, and poor judgment decisions from the past coalesce in just the right way to reactivate it. This is why A.A.'s experience says, "Once an alcoholic, always an alcoholic." A person's choice is not in being an alcoholic or not; it is in being a sober, recovering alcoholic or in being an out-of-control, practicing, using alcoholic. So the A.A. proviso that, once sober, "Don't take the first drink," follows in the most logical and reasonable way the practical implications of this aspect of the addiction reality.

Too many people in A.A. and addiction recovery have witnessed the horrifying experience of good friends who were once sober, sometimes for many years, losing everything, including their lives, after what many thought was only a minor slip, but was actually a relapse that they would never come back from, which killed them either literally or figuratively. It is a sad and terribly sobering experience, and a warning to never underestimate the power of an addiction or to take one's sobriety and recovery for granted.

Another way of looking at the "Feels Great" using dream is that addicted individuals in early recovery are still in varying stages and degrees of denial about being addicted, and the dreams are a mirroring and a part of this ongoing struggle and battle with acceptance of this painful reality on both a conscious and an unconscious level.

Later in recovery, especially after the first three years, a "Feels Great" using dream is more likely to be about an ego-identity that is slipping back into dangerous territory, where the deceptive whisperings of the Addiction-Shadow-Complex are beginning to have their manipulative, distorting influence once again. Sometimes the person is doing so well they begin to believe they are no longer addicted, that they can handle the alcohol, smoke the joint, roll the dice again without it becoming a problem. A.A., in its direct, simple, to-the-point way of looking at things, calls this "stinking thinking." Sometimes a person gets too far away from the initial excitement, attention, and reinforcement of early sobriety. Sobriety becomes boring and mundane and blasé and routine. The recovering individual isn't being regularly congratulated anymore for not drinking or using. Non-using is now normative. It becomes easy to become complacent. This is often accompanied by discontentment, moodiness, impatience, and general irritability. For family and friends, the addicted person can become very difficult to communicate with, to relate to, and to be around. A.A. calls this experience a "dry drunk." During these times, recovering individuals may be tempted by "Feels Great" using dreams.

If a recovering addicted person I'm working with has a "Feels Great" using dream, I see it as a warning that he or she may be slipping back toward potentially using again. Usually they are starting to minimize, rationalize, or deny important aspects of their lives, including the reality that they are still addicted individuals. Sometimes stresses are building up in their lives, and they are being tempted to revert back to their old, familiar coping mechanisms of the addictive behaviors. Sometimes they have consciously or unconsciously begun to dismantle their support system and recovery program. They've stopped going to A.A., stopped associating with other people in recovery, stopped talking with their sponsors, stopped working the Twelve Steps, stopped praying and meditating, stopped helping others toward recovery. Sometimes circumstances have changed things—a sponsor has moved away, a new job keeps one away from his or her favorite meeting, or the family has had to relocate, etc.

A "Feels Great" using dream offers an opportunity to stop and look at what is going on; to prevent a slip or a relapse; to reinforce what needs to be reinforced and strengthened as well as to let go of things that need not be held onto any longer; to reassess priorities, support systems, and one's recovery program, as well as one's current relationship to the Self or the Higher Power.

If a person with a good stretch of sobriety has a "Feels Great" using dream where both the dream ego and the waking ego are supportive of the using in the dream, then this person is of course at very high risk for relapse, and may need more intensive help and support and treatment intervention.

In most cases with significant sobriety when a person has a "Feels Great" using dream where the dream ego and the waking ego are at odds—where usually, but not always, the waking ego is less enthusiastic or even ambivalent about the using—this indicates that the person has been enjoying and appreciating, to some degree, the benefits of sobriety and does have an investment psychologically in recovery. The more healthy, normal ego may be returning to functioning and strengthening. It may be more able to discern and combat and counter the whisperings and lies and deceptions and temptations from the weakening Addiction-Shadow-Complex.

As you can see, in the "Feels Great" using dream there needs to be a weighing and discerning of what the dream ego's position is in relation to the waking ego's position, and a judgment made about the implications diagnostically, as well as what is called for therapeutically in each situation.

Just remember that any using dream must be viewed in the gestalt of the whole situation in working with the recovering individual. The dream needs to be viewed, like other dreams, in the very specific personal context and circumstances of the dreamer's life situation. Using dreams should not be taken as oracles or fate or prophecy, but as potentially helpful aids in understanding the current dynamics going on in that addicted person's situation.

Now I'd like to give a case example to illustrate how the "Feels Great" using dream can operate in the dynamics of an individual process.

A young white male, twenty-seven years old, whom I'll call Bill, came to see me for outpatient psychotherapy. He was addicted to alcohol, marijuana, and extremely destructive codependent romantic relationships. I usually don't try to work in outpatient psychotherapy or personal analysis with someone just getting sober or in very early recovery, because I have found it to be much less helpful and effective than going to A.A. (90 meetings in 90 days) or into an intensive primary treatment program for addiction, whether inpatient or day patient or even intensive outpatient (5 nights a week for 4 to 6 weeks). My experience is that early in recovery people need a great deal of repetitive daily structure, reinforcement, support, education, and encouragement if they are going to have a decent shot at getting and staying sober and truly recovering from their addiction. A once-, or at most twice-a-week, one-hour session is, in most cases, not nearly enough of what is needed. I do often encourage addicted individuals who initially come to me for help to first get sober and straight, to go to A.A., N.A., O.A., G.A., and/or an intensive primary treatment program for addiction. Then, after six months to a year or more of sobriety and recovery, to come back and see me for psychotherapy or personal analysis. My experience is that once the dust has settled, with a measure of sobriety under one's belt—once the cork is back in the bottle for a while and the person has had the opportunity to experience the initial benefits of getting sober and not indulging in the addictive behavior and to see how much gets better how quickly— the individual dynamics (persona, personal shadow, complexes, anima/ animus, developmental history, etc.) can then be more effectively explored and addressed in traditional psychotherapy or personal analysis.

Initially, as the study from the *Harvard Medical School Mental Health Letter* clearly indicates, the psychological effects of addiction are so mixed up and confused and distorting of the individual psyche and its dynamics that it is very difficult to sort out and clarify what is affecting what in the process. A good example of this distortion and confusion I observed personally when working as an inpatient addictions counselor at a primary treatment facility in Louisiana a number of years ago. As part of our admission procedures, we had our resident patients take an M.M.P.I. (Minnesota Multiphasic Personality Inventory) test the day they were admitted to the facility. Most of these people were still under the influence of drugs or alcohol when they were admitted; the substances were still significantly in their bodies. Many were going through medical detoxification.

What was particularly interesting and baffling to the treatment staff was that a great number of these people were scoring off the charts with extreme elevations on most of the psychopathology scales of the test. It looked like, under the influence of their addictions, they were the most disturbed, most mentally ill folks on the planet, and I guess in a way they were. Individuals would have off-the-chart elevations on numerous scales under Schizophrenia, Hypochondria, Depression, Hysteria, Sociopath, Borderline, Paranoia, Gender Identity, Phobia, Obsession/Compulsion, and Mania. The results made it seem as though an electrical wire in the system had shorted out on the test and the results were registering all over the place.

When the clinical director and counselors looked at the results, we knew there was something wrong. These scores could not be accurate and valid representations of the personality tendencies and issues in our patients—if so, then everybody had just about everything! So we discussed the issue and decided to also administer the M.M.P.I. test later in treatment, past detox and at least two weeks into recovery. The results were vastly different. People who previously were scoring off the charts now were scoring within the relatively normally expected ranges of psychological personality disturbance for individuals in initial recovery. The psychological influences and effects of an addiction should never be underestimated at any time in the process.

It was clear from this testing experience that the immediate effects metabolically of alcohol and drugs on these addicted people was to create a level of psychological disturbance and insanity that was almost unimaginable, and so greatly distorted the true nature of their personalities that they were almost unrecognizable as individuals. It also lends support to my contention that the Addiction-Shadow-Complex is so powerful and dominating a force in the psyche when it takes over that it literally obliterates the ability of people to truly be themselves in any kind of a healthy, normal way. It demonstrates Step One of A.A.—our powerlessness over alcohol and the out-of-control unmanageability of our lives. These are all different descriptions of the same phenomena.

In any case, I usually don't see people in their initial getting-sober stage of recovery, but I did agree at the time to see Bill. Two weeks into his sobriety, he reported having dreams that he was getting drunk and smoking grass and enjoying it. In his third week of recovery, he dreamt that he was driving and had been stopped by the police, who were checking for his license, which he didn't have because it was suspended for a D.W.I. (Driving While Intoxicated) offense. He talked his way out of being arrested or ticketed for driving illegally and was very pleased with himself that he had gotten away with it. The scene changed, and he was then on an airplane with his parents. He saw a girl he didn't know and decided he wanted to have a sexual affair with her on the spot. The impulsivity, need for immediate gratification, being above the law, and grandiose manipulation of circumstances were all obvious in these dreams. A.A. describes it as "self will run riot." It is clear that Bill at this time was having "Feels Great" using dreams for both his dreaming and waking ego. His commitment to sobriety was tenuous. He hadn't really surrendered his addicted ego to the Higher Power and was still very much under the influence and control of the Addiction-Shadow-Complex. He was trying to stay clean and sober with willpower, self-discipline, and ego control alone—what A.A. calls "white-knuckling it," which as we know never works if a person is truly addicted because he or she is trying to control what cannot be controlled by one's ego.

Bill started drinking and smoking pot again, and returned to a very destructive relationship with an old girlfriend after two months of sobriety. One of the conditions for my continuing to see Bill in psychotherapy was that he remain sober and straight and abstinent. I confronted him about our agreement. He missed several appointments and arrived late often. He reported putting together three weeks of sobriety and then began using again; this time it was out of control. I referred him to an inpatient intensive primary treatment program for addiction. He remained in treatment there for five weeks. When he returned to see me in outpatient psychotherapy, he was not going to A.A. or N.A. with any regularity, not working the Twelve Steps, hadn't gotten a sponsor, and wasn't attending his aftercare support group.

After sixty days of his most recent sobriety, he had completely stopped participating in any form of recovery or support system for his addiction problems. He reported having another dream about getting drunk, which he thoroughly enjoyed in his dream, and when he woke up he felt relieved that he could at least enjoy drinking in his dreams. Both his dream ego and waking ego continued to respond to his using dreams in a "Feels Great" way. Bill went back to one more A.A. meeting at my encouragement, and then he stopped altogether and started using both alcohol and marijuana again. He no-showed for the rest of his appointments with me and would not return my phone calls. His family and friends told me that his alcohol and drug use was even worse, and completely out of control. He told them he had no further interest in any help or treatment for his addictions.

Sadly, the Addiction-Shadow-Complex had sunk its teeth into Bill at this point and wasn't about to let him go again. The "Feels Great" using dreams were indications all along, even with his hit-and-miss sobriety, that he was in deep trouble because he had not had the necessary shift psychologically—the conversion experience, the relativizing of the ego taken in Steps One, Two, and Three of A.A. Without taking those first three steps—the neutralizing of the Archetypal Shadow/Archetypal Evil aspect of the addiction—all of Bill's other efforts were in vain, useless, and ineffective.

"FEELS AWFUL" USING DREAM REACTIONS

Typically, a using dream with a "Feels Awful" reaction by the dream ego and/or the waking ego occurs later in sobriety and recovery. Often, in the dream, the addicted person is tempted or slips or unknowingly drinks and uses. The reaction of the dream ego is not one of pleasure or enjoyment in using. The dream ego's reaction is more likely to range from being very upset and disappointed that one has lost his or her sobriety to at least a very uneasy, ambivalent feeling about it. Feelings of fear, failure, guilt, shame, disappointment, anxiety, and remorse are not uncommon. Many people report that in the dream itself they just felt awful about what had happened—thus my calling it a "Feels Awful" using dream. They felt terrible that they had slipped, relapsed, lost their sobriety, and were in danger of being swallowed up in the addiction once again.

Even if the dream ego takes some mixed pleasure in using in the dream, when the person wakes, his or her waking ego reaction is more significant. Most people's waking ego reactions to using in the dream are at first that they are very upset and feel awful that they may have relapsed. It takes some people a little time to realize it was a dream and not external reality; that they didn't actually drink or use. When they do realize this, they are tremendously relieved to know that their sobriety is still intact and that it was "only a dream," as people often say in their ignorance of the importance of dreams. But they then quickly begin to wonder what the using dream is all about, and why their psyche would send them such a dream. This is a great opportunity for these dreamers to look at where they are in their recovery process, the stresses in their lives, the strength of their support system, how well they are working the Twelve Steps, etc.

If a recovering addicted person has a "Feels Awful" using dream, diagnostically it is a good sign that the ego-identity of the person is more committed to sobriety and recovery and less to the addiction. The individual has progressed beyond the initial denial stage, is realizing the dangers of the addiction, is accepting the powerlessness over it on a much deeper level. The ego is not under as much of the addiction distortion and has internalized a true desire for sobriety. It is clear in these cases that sobriety is much more highly prized and valued, that the benefits of living sober are now something much more worth holding onto. A "Feels Awful" using dream is an indication, as they say in A.A., that "the program has taken hold."

In psychodynamic terms, it means the person is much more consciously invested in sobriety and healing; it indicates that the Archetypal Shadow/Archetypal Evil aspect of the Addiction-Shadow-Complex has been neutralized and the recovery battle can be fought on the human level, not the archetypal, with a healthier, more functioning ego to assist in the process. Now the psychological tools and resources of willpower, self-discipline, and ego control do have some power and say, and so can be of service to the Self (Higher Power) and can play a significant part in the thoughts, feelings, plans, decisions, and actions taken.

Treatmentwise, the "Feels Awful" using dream can have a number of potential meanings. It could be a reminder to the person that he or she is still addicted, if they have somehow forgotten or begun to rationalize away the fact. In this case it is a wonderful warning from the Self to take note and pay attention. It could also be a warning to the person that he or she is getting overconfident, inflated, and maybe thinking they can handle the addictive behavior after all, since they have learned and grown so much. A "Feels Awful" using dream can have the effect of bringing a person crashing back down to reality, regrounding and reminding one of all there is potentially to lose in a relapse. Perhaps such a dream is a caution, a warning about stresses that are building to dangerous levels, or that the person is not taking good enough care of him or herself and is more vulnerable than they realize.

The following is a case example to illustrate how a "Feels Awful" using dream operates. Tom was a 35-year-old white male who came to see me after four months of sobriety through his involvement with A.A. and N.A. He was in a professional graduate school at the time. He was addicted to alcohol and to almost every drug imaginable. He also was addicted to food, sex, and overly dependent relationships. At eight months of sobriety, he almost relapsed when on an airplane flight he got as close as holding the icing glass filled with Jack Daniels in his hands, reaching towards his mouth, before he put it down and did not drink. Shortly after this incident, Tom had a dream in which he felt overwhelmed, that everything was out of control. He was having difficulty writing his dissertation. His relationship with his girlfriend was miserable. He was drinking and drugging in the dream with complete abandon. The scene shifted and he suddenly jumped, leaped into a swimming-pool-sized fire ant hill, and woke up terrified, feeling scared and awful. Talk about being in over your head, with ants in your pants, whose fire could eat you alive. He got the message of the dream that he was at high risk to start using again, as a coping mechanism to handle the current stresses of his life that were building up to very dangerous levels. He realized he needed to beef up and strengthen his recovery program and support system; he needed to simplify, to reduce the stress factors in his life and to reprioritize. He did take the appropriate action, maintained his sobriety and recovery, and successfully graduated from his professional school. The last I heard of him was that he was sober and doing well.

Sometimes recovering alcoholic and addicted people have a drinking or using dream ten, twenty, or thirty years into sobriety, which seems to come out of nowhere and is not linked to anything that they can discern is going on or bothering them in their lives. Even if this using dream is not experienced as a "Feels Awful" using dream by the dream ego, or as somehow a warning of a serious threat to their sobriety, it is still, in most cases (of people I have spoken with), experienced by the waking ego subjectively as uncomfortable and a bit anxiety provoking. My guess is that these dreams occur periodically just to remind the recovering person that the addiction has not disappeared after all these years of sobriety, and that the Self or the Higher Power every once in a while taps him or her on the shoulder, through a using dream, just as a reminder to not forget the truth about addiction— that the indelible mark left by Archetypal Shadow/Archetypal Evil leaves a perpetual scar and vulnerability to the reactivation of the addiction. A.A. communicates this reality to its members both young and old in sobriety when it reminds them that they are potentially "only one drink away" (so to speak) from the unmanageability of their previous lives and the insanity of a reactivated addiction, which they have struggled so hard to avoid.

If there is a discrepancy in the ego states, in that the dream ego has a "Feels Awful" reaction to using in the dream and the waking ego has a "Feels Great" response, this incongruity, though rare, would indicate an urgent need to explore the nature of this unusual split. Is the person in some exceptional circumstance physically, psychologically, socially, or spiritually—a severe grief reaction, a clinical depression, some extreme loss, an existential crisis, a brain tumor, etc.—that would help explain the waking ego's uncharacteristic reaction? Whatever is discovered should be made more conscious and worked on through better integrating the new elements and issues into the picture psychologically.

"Somewhere-in-between" Using Dream Reactions

I've illustrated the "Feels Great" using dream with Bill's case and the "Feels Awful" using dream with Tom's case. The "Somewhere-in-between" using dream situation is where there is truly a mixture, a combination of varying reactions by both the dream ego in the using dream as well as the waking ego afterwards, with a variety of different reactions coming at different times from the same person. Sometimes he or she seems to be and truly is committed to sobriety and recovery, and this is reflected in the dreams. Sometimes the person is caught in the middle about it, ambivalent, and sometimes he or she is back again being swayed by the Addiction-Shadow-Complex, all reflected in the dreams.

I'd like to illustrate the "Somewhere-in-between" using dream situation with a case example of a young woman who worked with me over a relatively long period of time. Sally was a very attractive white female, twenty years old, in college when she first came to see me. Her drinking at the time was out of control and it was affecting her school performance, dating relationships, and her family. It was also putting her into some very dangerous and frightening situations physically and sexually. At my encouragement, she hooked up very positively with A.A., established sobriety, stabilized, and was feeling good about herself and her life.

At five months into her sobriety and recovery she dreamt that she was a slave to her A.A. sponsor and resented it very much. At seven months, she had not attended A.A. for six weeks, was in the emotional doldrums, and feeling very uneasy. Her A.A. sponsor had been out of town for a while, and Sally had begun going to bars again with her friends. She wasn't drinking, but she told me she had been thinking about it a lot, and part of her was more and more wanting to start drinking again. At this point, she had a dream where she started sipping on a gin and tonic, stopped, put the drink down, and watched it all night long as the ice melted and gradually watered the drink down. In the dream, she felt ambivalent, debated in her mind her desire to drink versus losing seven months of sobriety and all the things she had gained in the process.

Her dream ego was not upset that she had slipped and broken her sobriety by sipping the drink—in fact, the dream ego acted almost as if she were still sober and trying to make a decision, instead of actually already having crossed the line. Her waking ego's reaction was also not very upset that she had drunk and lost her sobriety in the dream. It also didn't seem concerned that she was seriously debating the question of returning to alcohol on a regular basis. What her waking ego was most concerned about was losing the seven months of sobriety and having other people be upset and disappointed in her. She also didn't like the idea of having to start over and work so hard again to put together another seven months of sobriety. She didn't say it, but what she really wanted was to be able to drink again without it counting against her sobriety. I've known others struggling with this issue of honesty, self- and communal deception, and trying to keep up a positive A.A. persona. Some denied slips, forgot them, or rationalized that they weren't significant enough to have constituted a loss of sobriety, so they continued the illusion of a longer record of sustained abstinence than they really had.

This is why A.A. emphasizes one day at a time with sobriety. Acknowledgment of accumulated sustained sobriety, with chips being given for numbers of years of abstinence on anniversaries of stopping drinking, is part of A.A.'s support and encouragement, but it is not what is most important or emphasized. Yesterday's sobriety no more guarantees today's or tomorrow's, than yesterday's binge means you can't get sober today and have the same change tomorrow. The insidious, manipulative, and reality-falsifying nature of the Addiction-Shadow-Complex is truly staggering. A.A. knows this aspect of addiction well when it cautions its members to remember that alcoholism is "cunning, baffling, and powerful!"[3]

I interpreted Sally's dream as a warning dream to Sally that her ambivalence about her sobriety was putting her in a weak, vulnerable, and confused place where her focus was on watching in a mesmerized way her drink water down all night long, and on what other people think of her. Is a watered-down drink somehow more acceptable than a full-strength one? Does the watered-down drink mirror, on the opposite side, her watered-down commitment to sobriety?

We talked about how the dream described her present psychological situation, where she wanted to maintain the benefits and gains of sobriety while at the same time she was dismantling her entire sobriety support system, putting herself in overwhelmingly tempting situations where the next easy step was to order that gin and tonic with the rest of her friends. Sally reminded me of that expression about people "wanting to have their cake and eat it too."

Sally responded well to the warning dream. She reinforced her support system again, maintained and continued her sobriety. She graduated successfully from college. She was two weeks away from a complete year of sobriety when she dreamt that she did begin drinking again, but she hid it from others and felt very upset and guilty about it in her dream. She had a "Feels Awful" using dream. Both her dream ego and waking ego were in agreement, and unhappy about having the using dream and hiding it. You can see in this dream how tenacious the Addiction-Shadow-Complex is, and how it never seems to give up trying to seduce the person back into the addiction using whatever means are available. When I explored the issue of hiding her drinking, she reported that her family knew she was alcoholic but that she still had not told her boyfriend and close friends about it. She was hiding it out of shame and embarrassment.

A month later, which turned out to be our last session together, after she'd been turned down for graduate school in a helping profession, she reported that she dreamt she had gotten drunk while taking care of others. She told me she had been wanting to drink some wine for some time now, and she hadn't been to A.A. meetings for several weeks. She started trying to convince me and herself that she was not really addicted to alcohol, but had only been abusing it, and now she felt she really could control it. I could not support her denial and rationalization of what was going on, and she left the session very unhappy with me for not colluding and agreeing with her self-deception. I felt sad and powerless and very concerned for Sally's well-being.

I received a letter from Sally three months later. In the letter, she indicated proudly that she had successfully resumed drinking and went into a lengthy explanation of how she was "doing fine" and, by implication, how off base and wrong I was about the nature of her drinking and my diagnosis of her as alcoholic. In the letter, almost as an afterthought, she mentioned that she was recovering from a terrible automobile accident heading home from a party. She wasn't wearing a seat belt and was almost killed. She required hundreds of stitches all over her face and body. She was medically recuperating at the time of the letter.

My guess is that she had been drinking at the party, which affected both her forgetting to use her seat belt and her handling of the car in the accident, but that it had not crossed her mind consciously that there was any connection. The ability of a person under the power of the Addiction-Shadow-Complex to delude, minimize, rationalize, confound, and deny some of the most obvious logical realities and consequences is a testament to its incredible ability to manipulate and control a person psychologically.

Sally's dreams indicated her ego-identity shifting back and forth between the Addiction-Shadow-Complex and sobriety. She had made it through the initial stage of denial, it seemed, and had put together over a year of sobriety; then her ego shifted back into delusion, denial, minimizing, and rationalizing, reflected in her thoughts, dreams, decisions, and actions. Sadly, the Addiction-Shadow-Complex kept calling her back to be under its domination and control. In some ways I believe Sally never could quite take Steps One, Two, and Three of A.A completely; there were always these reservations and the addicted ego never was able to collapse into the hands of the Higher Power or Self. There is a saying in A.A., "You must surrender to win" (Step One), and Sally could not surrender enough to win and keep her sobriety.

There is a postscript to Sally's story. I did run into her briefly a good while after the letter. She told me that she had continued drinking and it was again out of control and very self-destructive, and she knew it and wanted to stop, but just wasn't ready to take the step. Sally continued stuck in the middle, psychologically in between her desire to stop using and her desire to continue drinking, which of course is always exploited by the Addiction-Shadow-Complex to its advantage. Once again, in the A.A. Big Book, A.A. understands this dynamic oh so well when it says, "Half measures availed us nothing."[4]

I encouraged Sally to make sobriety her number one priority and focus, and emphasized how this was absolutely necessary for healing and recovery. She countered my encouragement by telling me she was seeing another therapist, a woman, and they were working on sexuality issues, not on her drinking problem. I had worked with Sally and others long enough to know that she wouldn't get very far working on her sexuality issues unless she could do it clean and sober. I wished her the best for the future, and hope she finds her way through grace to the healing power of the true Self.

When Sally was drinking, there was always a hostile, combative edge towards me, a kind of belligerence with a "nobody's gonna tell me what to do" attitude of defiance. It was a one-hundred-and-eighty-degree shift from her normally, most of the time, very positive transference toward me to a very negative, disdaining transference towards me. I'm sure the Addiction-Shadow-Complex saw me as its enemy, with my clear position opposing Sally's drinking. The Addiction-Shadow-Complex used this to create a pseudo power struggle between me and Sally, which was nothing more than a not-so-clever, transparent distraction away from the issue of sobriety and the ultimate consequences of Sally's returning to alcohol use. The power struggle was really between Sally and the Addiction-Shadow-Complex.

This kind of reaction is actually not unusual, and I have often experienced this negative transference reaction when my patients/clients who are recovering from addiction are about to or have begun participating again in their addictive behaviors.

In summary, it is important to consider dreams in dealing with the question of addiction. Dreams can help discern between abuse and addiction; they can point to important issues and dynamics involved in the addiction such as persona, personal shadow, false self, complexes, anima/animus, and True Self/Higher Power interactions. They can point to an ego-attitude position that can be used in diagnosis, prognosis, and treatment of the individual. Focusing especially on the dream ego and the waking ego reactions in using dreams can reveal a wealth of important information about where a person is in the recovery process, warn of relapse dangers, and encourage specific types of changes and interventions in the support system and recovery process.

Conclusion

In conclusion, I hope that this book has charted new territory and perhaps created a better map in trying to image, describe, and understand the psychodynamics of the phenomenon we know as addiction. My hope is that it will open up dialogue and discussion about what is and is not truly a psychological addiction. My hope is that the reasons for the effectiveness of A.A. and other Twelve Step programs in treating alcoholism and other addictions will be more clearly understood and appreciated by others outside of the A.A. community, especially by mental health professionals and the general public. My hope is that the many potential misunderstandings and misuses of the concept of Archetypal Shadow/Archetypal Evil will be avoided, and that it will be understood in the light in which it is offered. My hope is that addiction counselors and recovering individuals will more greatly appreciate the many helpful and often parallel concepts in Jungian psychology, especially the extraordinary potential of using dreams as a tool in the diagnosis and treatment of alcoholism and other addictions.

In the 1980s, I had a dream that I was assigned the job or task or role of carrying and transporting by hand a small, round container the size of a coffee cup, which was filled to the brim with the most potent, deadly, toxic concentration of archetypal evil imaginable, one tiny drop of which would destroy the whole world and all of humanity. My job was to walk very carefully, to keep my balance and not to slip or fall until I had carried this vessel without dropping or spilling any of its lethal contents to a preordained ritual site, where I was to gently place the container on the ground in the center of an eternally burning, moderate-sized wooden campfire, which would then be able to contain and neutralize the archetypal evil, as in a crucible, and which would protect humanity from being destroyed by it.

I feel as if I have the weight of the world on my shoulders as I walk and concentrate with all my might not to stumble or spill a drop.

I am terrified I will fail, as my body is losing strength. I am completely drenched in sweat from the tension and pressure and stress of the task at hand. I become totally exhausted, and am not sure I can make it. Finally, with every ounce of effort in my being, physically, emotionally, and spiritually, I successfully place the container vessel of evil in the center of the sacred fire, step back, and feel as if my life task has been accomplished.

I hope this dream is not about a grandiose inflation of my ego into a role of exaggerated self-importance. I believe the dream was an assignment from the Self in my individuation journey, which I didn't understand until I studied the Bill W./Carl Jung letters and began to handwrite this book. It has been years in its journey toward being published. My hope is that I have been able to place the Archetypal Shadow/Archetypal Evil of addiction where it can be seen and contained and neutralized in the eternal sacred fires of the Self and the Higher Powers of healing, light, and grace. My hope is that some of the veil of the Great Deceiver has been lifted for all to see and understand.

When all is said and done, I hope I am counted among the friends of A.A.

"spiritus contra spiritum"

Notes

INTRODUCTION

1. Ernest Kurtz and Katherine Ketchum, *The Spirituality of Imperfection: Storytelling and the Journey to Wholeness* (New York: Bantam, 1994), pp. 114-115.

2. Or, for example, as the combination of a physical allergy and a mental obsession hypothesized by Dr. William Silkworth, who wrote the original "The Doctor's Opinion" section of the Big Book of A.A. Neither will this book go into the considerable contributions of E. M. Jellinek, one of America's premier researchers into alcoholism, and his understanding of its stages and phases and the characteristics of the progressive deterioration of the addiction process.

3. Francis Kelly Nemerck, OMI, and Marie Theresa Coombs, Hermit, *O Blessed Night: Recovering from Addiction, Codependency and Attachment based on the Insights of St. John of the Cross and Pierre Teilhard de Chardin* (New York: Alba House, 1998), p. 5.

4. Gerald May, *Addiction and Grace: Love and Spirituality in the Healing of Addiction* (New York: Harper Collins, 1988), pp. 4-5.

5. *Ibid.*, p. 24.

CHAPTER 1: SETTING THE STAGE, THE BILL W. – CARL JUNG LETTERS

1. Reprinted from A.A. *Classic Grapevine* 35/6 (November 1978), pp. 26-29.

2. C. G. Jung, *The Collected Works of C. G. Jung*, trans. R.F.C. Hull, ed. H. Read, M. Fordham, G. Adler, Wm. McGuire, 20 vols. (Princeton: Princeton University Press, 1953-1979), vol. 18, § 558, 621. (Hereafter *CW.*)

3. Ernest Kurtz, *Not God: A History of Alcoholics Anonymous* (Center City, MN: Hazelden Educational Materials, 1979), p. 8.

4. *Alcoholics Anonymous, The Story of How Many Thousands of Men and Women Have Recovered from Alcoholism* (New York: Alcoholics Anonymous Word Service Inc., 1976), p. xxvii.

5. Reprinted from *Classic Grapevine* 35/6, pp. 30-31.

6. Such as Buddhist meditation practice, the spiritual exercises of Ignatius Loyola, Gestalt therapy, the Rule of St. Benedict, Kundalini yoga, Deepak Chopra's

work, Taoism, the Course in Miracles, Eckhart Tolle's *The Power of Now*, and so on.

7. Harry M. Tiebout, *Conversion as a Psychological Phenomenon* (New York: The National Council on Alcoholism, Inc.), p. 2.

8. *Classic Grapevine* 35/6, p. 31, italics mine.

CHAPTER 2: THE PSYCHODYNAMICS OF ADDICTION, DEVELOPMENT OF A TYPICAL ADDICTION PROCESS

1. Daryl Sharp, *Jung Lexicon: A Primer of Terms and Concepts* (Toronto: Inner City Books, 1991), p. 123.

2. C. G. Jung, "The Shadow," *CW* 9ii, § 14.

3. Linda Schierse Leonard, *Witness to the Fire: Creativity and the Veil of Addiction* (Boston: Shambhala, 1989).

4. *The World Book Encyclopedia*, 1993 edition, Vol. 18, p. 898.

5. Marion Woodman, "Holding the Tension of the Opposites" (audiotape).

CHAPTER 3: AN EXPLORATION OF ARCHETYPAL SHADOW/ ARCHETYPAL EVIL AS AN ESSENTIAL INGREDIENT IN ADDICTION

1. John Sanford, *Evil: The Shadow Side of Reality* (New York: Crossroad, 1988), p. 2.

2. *Ibid.*, p. 9.

3. C. G. Jung, "Individual Dream Symbolism in Relation to Alchemy," *CW* 12, § 44.

4. Sanford, *Evil*, p. 16.

5. James Hillman, ed., *Evil*, Studies in Jungian Thought Series (Evanston, IL: Northwestern University Press, 1967), pp. 7-10.

6. Sanford, *Evil*, p.17.

7. *Ibid.*

8. *Ibid.*

9. Lionel Corbett, *Psyche and the Sacred: Spirituality beyond Religion* (New Orleans, LA: Spring Journal Books, 2007), p. 153.

10. *Ibid.*, p. 160.

11. *Ibid.*, p. 150.

12. *Ibid.*, p. 165.

13. *Ibid.*, p. 174.

14. M. Scott Peck, *People of the Lie: The Hope for Healing Human Evil* (New York: Simon & Schuster, 1983).

15. *Ibid.*, p. 196.

16. *Ibid.*, p. 199.

17. Paul Woodruff and Harry A. Wilmer, eds., *Facing Evil: Confronting the Dreadful Power behind Genocide, Terrorism and Cruelty* (Chicago: Open Court, 1988), p. 4.

18. *Ibid.*, p. 24.

19. Peck, *People of the Lie*, p. 42.

20. *Ibid.*, p. 44.

21. Hillman, *Evil*, p. 14.

22. *Ibid.*, p. 16.

23. Jeffrey Burton Russell, *The Devil* (Ithaca and London: Cornell University Press), p. 23.

24. Woodruff and Wilmer, *Facing Evil*, p. 28.

25. Donald Kalsched, *The Inner World of Trauma: Archetypal Defenses of the Personal Spirit* (New York: Routledge, 1996).

26. *Ibid.*, p. 5.

27. Adolf Guggenbühl-Craig, *The Emptied Soul: On the Nature of the Psychopath* (Woodstock, CT: Spring Publications, 1980).

28. Marie-Louise von Franz, *C. G. Jung: His Myth in Our Time* (New York: C. G. Jung Foundation, 1975), p. 236.

29. C. G. Jung, "Symbols and the Interpretation of Dreams," *CW* 18, § 512.

30. Marie-Louise von Franz, *An Introduction to the Psychology of Fairy Tales* (Irving, TX: Spring Publications, 1978), p. 96.

31. *Ibid.*

32. C. G. Jung, "The Shadow," *CW* 9ii, § 19.

33. Clarissa Pinkola Estés, *Women Who Run with the Wolves: Myths and Stories of the Wild Woman Archetype* (New York: Ballantine, 1992), p. 63.

34. Von Franz, *Fairy Tales*, p. 125.

35. Linda Schierse Leonard, *Witness to the Fire: Creativity and the Veil of Addiction* (Boston: Shambhala, 1989), p. 4.

36. Cited in Hillman, *Evil*, pp. 6-7.

37. *Ibid.*, p. 7.

38. Mario Jacoby, Verena Kast, and Ingrid Riedel, *Witches, Ogres and the Devil's Daughter: Encounters with Evil in Fairy Tales* (Boston: Shambhala, 1992), p. 24.

39. *Ibid.*, p. 38.

40. In Hillman, *Evil*, p. 89.

41. *Ibid.*, pp. 94, 96.

42. Kent and Maria Carr, *Unraveling Collective Confusion: Archetypes and Issues* (Cornville, AZ: AI Publications, 2001).

43. Estés, *Women Who Run with the Wolves*, p. 248.

44. Leonard, *Witness to the Fire*, p. 18.

45. Woodruff and Wilmer, *Facing Evil*, p. 61.

46. In Hillman, *Evil*, p. 100.

47. *Ibid.*, p. 107.

48. *Ibid.*

49. Ernest Kurtz, *Not God: A History of Alcoholics Anonymous* (Center City, MN: Hazelden Educational Materials, 1979), pp. 13-14.

50. Liliane Frey-Rohn, "Evil from the Psychological Point of View," in Hillman, *Evil.*

CHAPTER 4: THE HEALING PROCESS OF RECOVERY THROUGH THE TWELVE STEPS OF A.A.

1. Ernest Kurtz, *Not God: A History of Alcoholics Anonymous* (Center City, MN: Hazelden Educational Materials, 1979), p. 61.

2. Linda Schierse Leonard, *Witness to the Fire: Creativity and the Veil of Addiction* (Boston: Shambhala, 1989), p. 36.

3. *Ibid.*, p. 185.

4. Cited in *ibid.*

5. *Twelve Steps and Twelve Traditions* (New York: Alcoholics Anonymous World Services, Inc., 1972).

6. Kurtz, *Not God*, p. 125.

7. Daryl Sharp, *Jung Lexicon: A Primer of Terms and Concepts* (Toronto: Inner City Books, 1991), p. 123.

8. John Sanford, *Healing and Wholeness* (New York: Paulist, 1977), p. 57.

9. Eckhart Tolle, *The Power of Now: A Guide to Spiritual Enlightenment* (Novato, CA: New World Library, 1999), p.127.

10. Marion Woodman, *Addiction to Perfection: The Still Unravished Bride* (Toronto: Inner City Books, 1985), p. 31.

11. Kurtz, *Not God*, p. 61.

12. Leonard, *Witness to the Fire*, p. 323.

13. C. G. Jung, "On the Psychology of the Unconscious," *CW* 7, § 35.

14. Jolande Jacobi, *The Way of Individuation* (New York: New American Library, 1967), p. 40-41.

15. Leonard, *Witness to the Fire*, p. 335.

16. *Ibid.*, p. 351.

17. "Treatment of Alcoholism, Part II," *The Harvard Medical School, Mental Health Letter* 4/1 (July 1987), p. 2.

CHAPTER 5: "USING DREAMS" OF RECOVERING ALCOHOLIC AND ADDICTED INDIVIDUALS

1. Reed A. Morrison, "Dream Mapping in Chemical Dependency Recovery," *Alcoholism Treatment Quarterly* 7/3 (1990).

2. James Hall, *Jungian Dream Interpretation: A Handbook of Theory and Practice* (Toronto: Inner City Books, 1983), p. 30.

3. *Alcoholics Anonymous: The Story of How Many Thousands of Men and Women Have Recovered from Alcoholism* (New York: Alcoholics Anonymous World Services Inc., 1976), pp. 58-59.

4. *Ibid.*, p.59.

Index

Milton Keynes UK
Ingram Content Group UK Ltd.
UKHW041458140224
437827UK00001B/189